Sweet Daughter of Eve

bush PUBLISHING & associates

"*Sweet Daughter of Eve* shines a light on child abuse—the pervasive, often hidden maltreatment of our most vulnerable population. While the author endured much of her abuse alone, she did find support and solace through a beloved, supportive adult, and in later years, her developing Faith and her Faith community. I would encourage all social workers and child advocates to read this book both for the insight it offers into the trauma child abuse victims face and as a tool for early intervention. Child abuse survivors can take from the book that there is hope. Survivors may suffer long-term impacts of their abuse, but like the author, they, too, can successfully become resilient."
Lauren Anderson, LMSW, ACM-SW
(Licensed Master Social Worker, Accredited Case Manager)

"This book will make you cry, will make the spirit of justice rise up inside of you, and it will make you smile with the Hope of the Living God. *Sweet Daughter of Eve* makes us aware of child abuse possibly happening next door to us, without us ever knowing. Through all the trials and trauma the author experienced, there is so much tenderness and love so evident in her life. Please read this and use it to understand what child abuse survivors go through. I am proud of how resilient and emotionally healthy Claire is. Her writing is beautiful and pulls you in her story."
Fibi Davidson, LPC

"In both the triumphant and the tragic events detailed in *Sweet Daughter of Eve*, the reader gets to experience the many Biblical references lift from the pages and into the heart. So often I hear believers and non-believers lament how distant the Holy Scriptures can sometimes feel, as if they come from another world and are for some other nation long forgotten. The reality is God's Word is ever-present and ever-speaking right where we are, in both times of light and times of darkness. The Pastoral effect Claire Ostrander will have upon her audience is one that will be both an immediate and gradual blessing. Listen to the Lord with her, and discover your Biblical story as you experience the pages of hers."
Pastor Ross Wheeler

Sweet Daughter of Eve

Claire Ostrander

bush PUBLISHING & associates

Dedication

To the man, the myth, the legend.
Often imitated, never duplicated:
Uncle Tommy.

Table of Contents

Acknowledgements

I would like to take a moment to give my heartfelt thanks to all of those who provided their unconditional love and support for me throughout the painstaking yet rewarding process of turning Sweet Daughter of Eve from a mere dream into reality.

Thank you, God, for showing up. You are never late; you are always on time. You made beauty from ashes in helping me share my story.

Next, I thank my husband, soulmate, lifelong partner, and best friend, Nathan. Words fall short to adequately express the depth of my eternal gratitude and love for you. I will try my very best, though. Nathan, you have stood by my side in my early, failed attempts to write this book. You stood by my side as I began to let go of this dream. Most importantly, you stood by as I dusted off my laptop and tried again. Even after the book was finished, you stood by my side and, hand in hand, we waited for God to reveal to us how this was all going to work. Now, as I cross the finish line, you continue to stand in the same place: right by my side. I love you more than words can ever describe!

Thank you to my wise-beyond-his-years, 11-year-old son, Luke. You are "my light", Luke and as my firstborn son, you officially put into motion a new legacy of Christ, hope, and love. Your unwavering enthusiasm for the book did not go unnoticed. Even at such a young age, you showed such interest in your mom's book. Your involvement and support mean the world to me.

Next, I would like to recognize those individuals who offered me unending love and support, as I embarked upon my journey of writing Sweet Daughter of Eve. In no particular order, these people are Jessica Sprecher, Debbie Sehorn, Lauren Anderson, Fibi Davidson, Brianna Belliconish, Julie Ostrander, Patrick Rhodes, Marnie Murray, Alicia Davis, Lisa Logdson, Regina Givi, Cheri Collins, Patricia Chenet, Daniel Waajid, and the entire Givi School of Music community, The Bible Chapel Robinson campus, Shannon Angelo, Denise Gallagher, and Kim Rodrigues.

Prologue

Sweet Daughter of Eve tells the story of child abuse, beginning in early childhood through adolescence, and addresses the long-term effects of said abuse into adulthood. My story was written to raise a greater awareness of child abuse, particularly for the covered-up cases. Even so, *Sweet Daughter of Eve*, as you will soon see, is so much more than that. It's the beautiful story of how God gave me a person (my beloved Godfather Tommy) to look out for me and protect me throughout the tumultuous experiences and effects of a life of child abuse.

The story flows as a back-and-forth model between my life of child abuse (each coupled with relevant scriptures) to uplifting, authentic copies of the vivid artwork sent with each letter from Uncle Tommy—my godfather and lifetime advocate.

Most importantly, *Sweet Daughter of Eve* includes relevant scriptures throughout each instance of child abuse to emphasize the book's theme that there is no trial that cannot be addressed through God's Word. Many scriptures are used in conjunction with the beautiful art my godfather sent me throughout my lifetime as an encouraging reminder that when God said he will never leave nor forsake us, He meant it. Even though I wasn't aware of these scriptures during most of my unspeakable episodes of child abuse, it doesn't mean the scriptures were not there. John 1:1-5 says, "In the beginning was the Word, and the Word was with God, and the Word was God. He was with God in the beginning. Through him, all things were made; without him, nothing was made that has been made. In him was life, and that life was the light of all mankind. The light shines in the darkness, and the darkness has not overcome it."

In other words, the Word of God transcends the parameters of space and time. It is the personification of God himself before God even created the world, and it brings a light that will unfailingly outshine the darkest depths and valleys of life.

Given that the Word of God already existed before it was written, we know that the Word of God surrounds us. As such, God's Holy Spirit is always with us.

Sweet Daughter of Eve proves this point by applying relevant scriptures to each scene of abuse throughout the book. You see, you don't need to be reading the Bible for the Word of God to be with you. In fact, you don't even need to have a Bible in your room or even in your hand for the Word of God—the essence of God and His Holy Spirit—to be with you. The Word of God always has been and always will be. We need to know the Word of God to live out God's plans and purposes and make us more aware of His constant presence.

This little girl wasn't taught the Word of God, and she grew into adolescence still not knowing the Word of God. Now, as an adult with a family of my own, I have found Jesus and learned the Word of God for myself. As I look back on my life of child abuse and apply the word of God to each experience, it tells me—and I pray it shows you—how God was with me the entire time regardless of whether I knew Him or not. God is no respecter of persons, so if he was always with me, I know he is also always with you. Indeed, God has always been with you, even in the times you didn't feel Him. It is my prayer that *Sweet Daughter of Eve* will give you a greater revelation of God's unending presence throughout every moment of your life.

While *Sweet Daughter of Eve* is the story I was born to write, I know God has so much more for me. This is only the beginning. If you have ever experienced any type of abuse or if you are struggling to find God's purpose for your life, I pray that *Sweet Daughter of Eve* will be the beginning of a new journey for you toward healing and hope.

I am honored that you have chosen to read my story. May God bless you!

Love in Christ,

Claire Ostrander

Introduction

"See to it that you do not despise one of these little ones. For I tell you that their angels in heaven always see the face of my Father in heaven."
-Matthew 18:10 [NIV]

I looked down at the scuff marks on my ballet slippers as I placed one foot in front of the other, feeling more and more desensitized with each step I took.

I would have changed into walking shoes and street clothes had I known that Mother would leave me on the side of the road on the drive home from dance class.

Yet, there I was on the side of one of Marietta, Georgia's busiest streets wearing a leotard and ballet tights with my dance bag slung around my shoulder. Mother had forced me to walk the entire five miles home. I even passed a cemetery en route.

This was just another day in my life as Mother's daughter. It was not a life for the faint of heart. It was a constant war zone, and at eleven years old, I was living on the frontlines.

"Just as one candle lights another and can light thousands of other candles, so one heart illuminates another heart and can illuminate thousands of other hearts."

-Leo Tolstoy

Part One
A Subtle Start

Chapter One

Her Dying Wish

The whispering lulls of the hospital room ventilator had become so commonplace to Miriam that she no longer heard its sound. At seventy-four, she had lived a good life as a respected journalist, and she was eager to join her husband who had gone to be with the Lord over a decade ago. John was an English professor at the University of Georgia for over twenty years. Writing was a gift in the family. Not all received it, but those who did learned early in life. Her son, Leonard, had inherited this gift, and his daughter, Suzanne, also received it. In fact, Suzanne was the one that had kept her alive until she could make her wishes known.

Miriam saw the great potential in Suzanne and spent much of her lifetime discussing this gift with her godfather, Tommy. Both Miriam and Tommy were well aware of the issue with Suzanne's mother. Her name was Darlene, and she was a dangerous woman. There was nothing she could say to her son, as he had become utterly embedded as an enabler to her narcissistic personality. So Miriam spent those long, troubled nights on the phone with her son's best friend and Suzanne's godfather, Tommy, expressing her concern. Miriam felt that Suzanne's creativity and powerful imagination as a writer could quite possibly become curtailed under the yoke of Darlene's abusive behavior. She wasn't ready to leave yet—she had to speak to Tommy.

After what seemed like hours, the hospice nurse escorted Tommy into Miriam's hospital room, where he sat by her bedside. Miriam had already spoken with everybody else she needed to speak with. He was last on her list. She looked Tommy in the eye, and he anticipated the words before they left her lips.

It was her last sentence spoken on Earth—her final, dying wish. With her last breath, she looked into Tommy's eyes and said:

"Watch over Suzanne."

"Defend the oppressed. Take up the cause of the fatherless."
-Isaiah 1:17 [NIV]

Chapter Two
A Time to Be Born

On May 24th, 1981, I—Suzanne Elizabeth Thompson—was taken out of eternity and placed into time. It was my time to be born.

Some say I entered this world unarmed; some say I didn't have a chance. But God says I have a purpose, and my purpose is to tell my story.

"To everything there is a season, and a time to every purpose under Heaven… A time to be born."
-Ecclesiastes 3:1 [NIV]

Chapter Three

Porcelain Doll

> *"Oh that I would have the wings of a dove! I would fly far away and be at rest; far from the tempest and the storm."*
> *-Psalm 55:6 & 8*

In my case, my child abuse started out subtly. My biological mother had severe narcissistic personality disorder; a curious condition passed down from generations that robbed her of the freedom to enjoy and love her daughter. Daughters were looked at as competition by women with NPD. To this day, I hold only profound compassion and love (from afar) for my biological mother. The only thing I ever really blamed her for was never getting help. That's where she truly went wrong.

In my youngest years, Mother was not quite the monster she later built herself up to become. In those days, Mother—unable to truly love her daughter—looked at me as a mere accessory.

"Look what I made!"

Anything I did or didn't do was always a reflection of Mother. "Don't you dare get dirty. Don't you dare run on the beach and get sand on you. Don't you dare let me see your hair unbrushed. Don't. You. Dare."

My story begins not so horrifically. After all, some of the greatest tragedies take time to unfold.

For the most part, I was like a living porcelain doll. If she could, she would have placed a "Designs by Darlene" tag on my butt when I was born.

One of my earliest memories of her abuse was around age four. I remember we were all out on a boat that day with friends. (This was back when Mother still had friends.) When we reached a certain depth at the lake, the speedboat stopped, and my older brother and I put on our life jackets and jumped in.

To this day, I'm not sure what exactly I ate (or what lake water I swallowed), but no longer than five minutes after jumping into the lake, I realized that it was time to find a toilet. Oh yes, it was time to go #3: Montezuma's Revenge.

Even at four, I knew it wasn't a big deal. I mean, it happens, right? It's not like I pooped my pants or went all over their boat. After I went to the boat restroom, I went to find Daddy. He was the one who I knew loved me. "Daddy, Daddy, I have the poopies. Can you make it go away?"

I knew what his response was going to be even before he replied. "Oh no, sweetie. Tell you what, why don't you find your mother. She will help find something to make you feel better, sweet girl."

After all, Mother made all the decisions.

I just stared at my Daddy with big, blue, disappointed eyes. "Okay, Daddy," I reluctantly replied.

The walk back down the steps to the first floor seemed to take an eternity.

I found Mother.

When I told Mother what was happening, she slapped on a face of synthetic sympathy as if to say, *"Don't you worry about a thing, baby girl, Mommy's here."*

Yeah, right.

I wasn't sure what she was up to (I never was), but it was never anything good.

Surprisingly, Mother came back down with some Pepto Bismol. Ah, the smooth pink taste of bismuth delight. I had to admit, I didn't necessarily hate the taste of this curious pink concoction, so I was humorously delighted to be taking a swig.

All her friends were around, so she made sure to see to it that I waited at least fifteen minutes before going back to play in the lake. I waited and returned to the lake, and we played for the rest of the day. I kept wondering what the catch was. Mother wouldn't just help me out of the genuine love in her heart from a mom to a daughter.

It usually never took too long for the other shoe to drop. Once we had packed up for the day and were all back in the car, Mother made it a point to turn to me slowly. With an eerily unsettling voice, she decided she would shame me and said coldly, "Now, Suzanne, I want you to know that there's no way that was kept a secret between you and me. I know that the minute we left, Mrs. Wilpers went and told everybody on that boat, including your friends, that 'Suzanne had diarrhea.'"

Wow. It's like my butt was suddenly on trial in a court of law. Thanks for having everybody aware of my indigestive indiscretions, Ma. It was only fair to shame me in this department, seeing as her butt apparently smelled like the entire Summer Breeze collection from Bath & Body Works.

Even at age four, I looked at her as if I were the adult and she was the child.

How she hated it when I did that!

"Even in laughter, the heart may ache, and rejoicing may end in grief."
-Proverbs 14:13 [NIV]

Now, when it comes to Tommy, there's one thing you should know: Long before he made his vow of protection over my life, Tommy and I had always been kindred spirits. It was that same free-loving spirit that Miriam wished to keep protecting. It's also what made Tommy eagerly comply to fulfill this lifelong promise.

It seemed like it was never long after any significant trauma in my life that my beloved godfather, Tommy, would soon check in on me. Before Miriam's passing, it was out of love. Following her last wishes, the acts were now out of both love and commitment to his promise.

May 24th 1984,
My Dearest Sweet, Sweet Suzanne,

It seems like just yesterday I received the telephone call from your father, and your Mimi and I rushed to the hospital to meet baby Suzanne for the very first time. I know God has wonderful things in store for you! Keep laughing and keep smiling that bright smile, baby girl. I'm pretty convinced you could hang the moon.

With Deep Love,
Uncle Tommy

The Light She Tried to Dim

By some unknown grace of God, I was actually a very happy child. It's almost like the darker things got, the brighter my light shone. Even compared to somebody with a non-abusive upbringing, I would typically stand out in a crowd. I was often remembered as the happy, smiley, bright little girl.

Sometimes, God works miracles that are so inexpressibly mysterious you cannot help but fall more and more in love with him.

As for Mother, well, she deeply resented this happiness.

Who did I think I was, becoming a free spirit when she never knew how to be? Was I actually daring to enjoy life? This was nowhere near the plans she had for us. I was a deviant, and this certainly had to stop.

So, she tried to dim my light by constantly mocking the brightest quality about me: my cute giggle.

Before I knew it, the next time a joke was told or I found humor in the world (as I always did), she made it a point to comment that my laugh sounded like that of a hyena's.

I was so confused. Everybody loved my little laugh. Why couldn't Mother? I decided to continue being myself around others, and while I had planned to subdue the happiness level of my laughter whenever she was around, it turns out my joy could not be so easily hidden. I was still young, but I was old enough to know that I was not obliged to stifle my joy for one person.

Mother did not like that.

"You are the light of the world. A city built on a hill cannot be hidden. Neither do people light a lamp and put it under a bowl. Instead, they put it on its stand, and it gives light to everyone in the house. In the same way, let your light shine before others, that they may see your good deeds and glorify your Father in heaven."
-Matthew 5:14-16 [NIV]

It wasn't long until Mother began mocking other expressions of my joy.

Something that I did at a very young age is what I like to call "wings." The "wing" maneuver is demonstrated when surges of unexpected joy arise from within my spirit and somehow physically translate into flapping both hands and opening my mouth like a little bird. I was little. It was cute. To this day, when I see my youngest express himself this way, it brings my heart such joy.

One of Mother's common techniques was constantly deriding these precious moments of pure joy in a little girl. She realized she could get away with mocking my joy if it was presented in the context of somebody else saying it.

For instance: "Suzanne, while I was outside in the parking lot waiting for you this afternoon, one of the boys in your class said, 'Mommy, what's wrong with Suzanne? Why does she do that with her arms?' The mom laughed and said, 'Oh honey, nothing's technically wrong with her. That's just what she does when she's excited.' Isn't that a funny story?"

Hilarious, I guess.

Apparently, it was such a funny story that it was told my entire life. To this day, I have my doubts as to if that conversation actually occurred or not.

The happiest I have ever seen Mother is when she subtly mocks me. After all, how could her intentions be evil? The story brought her so much joy.

Although I never liked hearing the story, a part of me was happy that she could finally find joy in something.

"...Do not provoke or irritate or exasperate your children, so they will not lose heart and become discouraged or unmotivated with their spirits broken."
-Colossians 3:21 (AMP)

May 24th, 1985,
Happy Happy Birthday to My Sweet Suzanne!

How are you already five years old, baby girl? I heard from your dad recently, and I wanted to be the one to tell you that we are all going on vacation together soon to Hunting Island! Get ready, Little Miss Sunshine! We will have the time of our lives. Talk to you soon, my shining light.

All My Love Under the Sun,
Uncle Tommy

"Among those whom I like or admire, I can find no common denominator. But among those whom I love, I can: All of them make me laugh."
-W.H. Auden

Chapter Five

"My Mommy Says…"

"Children are a heritage from the LORD, offspring a reward from him."
-Psalm 127:3 [NIV]

Scripture is filled with examples of how much God values children; He views them as an asset of the utmost worth. In my family, I was considered a liability—a nuisance. I was to be seen and not heard. If the Word of God says children are a "heritage from the Lord" and a "reward," not only should children naturally bring joy and pleasure, but adults should learn much from their inquisitive minds and trusting spirits. Instead of viewing children as a distraction or a nuisance, we should see them as an opportunity to shape the future. We have no right to treat children as an inconvenience when God values them so highly.

At the next stage of my progressive child abuse, Mother realized it was time to begin implementing verbal abuse to the menu. After all, it was just words, right? Sticks and stones, right?

Her first plan of attack was to use stories to devalue my very existence.

One of her favorites involved a comment my brother made when I was two. According to Mother's accounts, I was supposed to be a boy, and she had told James that she picked out the name "Matthew." After two years of my existence, James innocently said, "Mom, Suzanne's great and all, but when is Matthew getting here?"

Sure, okay, funny. Cute, even. Yet again, something was unnerving about the Cheshire Cat-like smile glued on Mother's face whenever she told the story. Why did she tell the story so often? Why did she continue to tell it far into my adulthood? Indeed, I would be the one looked at as aggressive if I questioned her motives.

After all, she's just telling a funny story. Lighten up!

Mother devised additional ways of devaluing my existence through yet another story: The story of my birth. Typically speaking, most non-abusive mothers will craft a lovely story about the moment they first met their child. Even if a mother has not told such an account to her child(ren), it's safe to assume a non-abusive mother would not continuously tell her child the story about how awful an experience it was bringing her child into the world.

I'm a mom of two, and I know the process isn't all sunshine and roses, but hey—I signed up for it. For me, it was completely worth it. Even if a mom shares her struggles, don't let that be the *only* thing a mother tells her child about their birth. Either say nothing, or, if you dare include suffering, you better be prepared to say how much it was all worth it!

All I got was a lifetime of how Mother asked, "Can I please have pain medicine?" and was told, "So sorry, sweetie, you got to the hospital too late!" So, as a result, Mother was forced to give birth with no pain medicine. What a horrible experience for her! The end.

Yet, how dare I question Mother's motives? After all, she was in a lot of pain during childbirth; she deserves to tell that story that way.…

I'm so glad my entrance into the world caused so much pain and nothing else.

Don't think I didn't notice her face when she told that story, too. It was the polar opposite of the Cheshire Cat grin that came with the stories that made fun of me. The chilling grimace her face made when she told the story of my birth told me more than any words ever could.

March 13, 1986,
My Dearest Suzanne,

I saw this piece of art on a greeting card, and it instantly made me think of you and your creative, free spirit. No particular reason, but I wanted to send some love your way and let you know that I love you and I am thinking about you. I can't wait to see all of the wonderful things the Lord will do in your life.

I remain, forever, your most fervent fan.

With Deep Love,
Uncle Tommy

P.S. - I think one of my favorite feelings is whenever I laugh together with you. Halfway through I simply realize how much I enjoy your existence.

Hunting Island

" Now the Lord is Spirit, and where the Spirit of the Lord is, there is freedom."
-2 Corinthians 3:17 [NIV]

Vacations were always special for me. Every kid enjoys the idea of a fun trip. At such a young age, I didn't realize what I was experiencing was abuse; I looked at it as "the bad stuff." I suppose that made it that much harder when "the bad stuff" dared to rear its ugly head at Disney World or the beach.

I hadn't quite figured out that child abuse—"the bad stuff"—didn't take vacations.

Nevertheless, my Daddy came in at 6 A.M., woke me up, and lovingly carried me down the stairs while I was still wearing my pajamas. This was my favorite part of every vacation: Daddy waking me up and carrying me to the car. I was still his little girl. It was him and I against Mother. Brother was Mother's golden child. I had my Daddy; all was fair in my world.

The car trips were always fun. Mother bought many things for Brother and me to play with and keep us entertained. So many toys. With all of these toys, there had to be love tucked in the gaps somewhere. I just wasn't looking hard enough. I would find it.

As a family tradition, we typically stopped at Denny's about two hours into the journey to have breakfast and change into our regular clothes. Mother was letting me wear my pajamas for a moment in public! What a treat. Not too much longer, and I'll find that love. I was sure of it.

After breakfast, we hit the road again headed onward to our destination, which happened to be Hunting Island this time. It's important to note that this vacation wasn't like any other vacation. This one was special because my beloved Uncle Tommy would be there. No wonder I slept like a baby in the car. I had been so excited thinking about going to the beach with Uncle Tommy that I did not sleep very well at night for an entire week. Although school was out for the summer, Mother put concealer underneath my eyes that week. She couldn't let anybody see anything out of order when it came to that free-spirited daughter of hers.

Finally, we arrived at our destination. I could smell the familiar scent of the salty air, and I heard the luxurious crashes of waves on the beach. Welcome to Hunting Island.

It's safe to say that Hunting Island will forever be locked in Mother's memory bank as nothing short of a disgrace and a travesty to all the plans she had for me. You see, Hunting Island is where I finally allowed myself the freedom to run on the beach. Like a wild horse trapped for years in a stall, Hunting Island ignited something within the deepest part of my soul, and I finally gave it the freedom to run free.

Hunting Island was my cute giggle. Hunting Island was my happy wings. Hunting Island was my creative writing, my magnificent imagination, my overlooked singing voice, and my inexplicable ability to express myself through art and music. Hunting Island was the beauty that Mother had tragically missed when I took my first breath of air and cried my first cry.

Hunting Island was, quite unexpectedly, the personification of my innermost soul. Hunting Island needed to get out and praise the Lord, because it finally did.

The relationship between my quenched spirit and Hunting Island became abundantly clear to Tommy and Mimi one afternoon when we all walked on the beach right before dusk. God is such a rightful showoff, for he painted the most indelible hues of bright orange, pink, and blue on the horizon that night.

Suddenly, Tommy and I—the kindred spirits that we were—just looked at each other with a grin. It was uncanny how he and I could often communicate with one another with the exchange of a single glance. In an instant, without any words spoken, we both took off running as if we were untamed horses released into the wild. Set free from the imprisonment chains, released from all emotional bondage and associated home cuffs.

The spontaneous foot race had begun, and boy was I whooping Uncle Tommy's behind! Never mind the fact that I was roughly a quarter of a century younger. We were two free spirits embarking upon a spontaneous foot race. It was up to him to keep up.

To this day, I remain uncertain of how long I kept running. Something was unleashed within me, and I couldn't stop. Tommy had stopped long before me, but I had experienced something I never knew was within the realm of possibility. I experienced true happiness. Just before the sunset that day, I almost forgot about the bad stuff. No, I completely forgot about the bad stuff. My, how exhilarating of an experience it all was.

While I would love to say that I ran miles ahead of everybody and went entirely out of sight, I did not. It may have felt that way, but in reality, it wasn't. I probably would have if I knew where the heck our hotel was, but alas, I knew to keep at least Uncle Tommy within earshot of my spirited sprint.

What happened next has been forever grafted in my mind as well as Uncle Tommy's, Mimi's, Brother's, and Mother's memories. The memory was there for each person, but it processed much differently for me, Uncle Tommy, and Mimi than it did for Brother and Mother.

The best way I can describe the next scene is to refer back to the famous cartoon series Charlie Brown. Whenever a spiritless adult or dull person spoke, there was a certain sound that played. You know the sound.

When I finally decided to allow my eardrums to transition from the exhilarating vibrations of the calming seashore to whatever madness this next sound was, I realized it was no one other than my brother, James, chasing me down the beach like a mad mother hen soaked from head to toe.

Bye-bye freedom.

"Suzanne… Suzanne… Suzanne… SUZANNE!!!"

I realized, at some point, I would have to acknowledge his existence.

"Whaaaaaaaat?"

"Suzanne! What have you been doing running out here in the sand and the dirt like some wild animal? Mother specifically told us *not* to run on the beach and *not* to get dirty. Look at you—you're a mess! Wait until Mother sees this!"

I just silently gazed at him as if I were the adult and he was a mere child.

How he hated it when I did that.

Not long after, good ole Uncle Tommy crossed the finish line and gave me a spirited high-five and a hug I will remember for the rest of my life.

"Never lose that spirit, baby girl, you hear me?"

"Tommy?" I whispered.

"Yes, love?"

"I'm so happy you're my godfather."

I could see tears welling up in his eyes as he responded, "Kid, you could lasso the moon."

On the walk home, Uncle Tommy and I dumped an entire bucket of sand on the unsuspecting, well-groomed brother James. What a mess he was.

Part Two
Time to Turn Up the Heat

Chapter Seven

Well, There's Always Christmas....

Many nights, I would lie awake while staring outside my window, trying my best to sort through whatever myriad of trauma the day had brought. Many times, the only thought that would ever get me to finally fall asleep was the thought of Christmas. "There's always Christmas," I would say to myself.

The idea of the next Christmas (no matter how far away it was) comforted me on many listless nights because I learned at an early age that it was the only way I could ever possibly feel loved by Mother, Brother James, and eventually even my dearest father.

I sometimes pictured them as a large metaphorical wallet. With Mother and Father as a "wallet", I knew I could never get the authentic kind of love, so I merely reminded myself that I received love in a way that was different from all of my friends.

So, if it truly was love, then why did it always make me so sad?

Since presents were such an essential thing for Brother and me, if there ever was a moment on any Christmas morning where I perceived Brother

James getting more presents than me (either in quantity or quality), it was like my heart crumbled to pieces and fell onto the floor. I didn't care about the actual gifts. I never had. However, if he received more than me, it must have been their way of showing that they do not love me as much as James that year. After all, gifts were love in that home.

I will never forget one year when we were going through pictures taken on Christmas morning and the camera happened to capture this moment in time for me. The minute I saw the picture, I knew exactly what was going on in my mind.

Of course, Mother was none the wiser. I remember her looking at that picture and scolding me for daring to show anything but joy at a time of the year when they could shine as parents. I'll never forget the look on her face when she saw the picture. She could not—would not—accept that I had any type of emotion other than joy and love at all of the so-called "love" surrounding me.

The only way she could cope with the look on my face in that picture was not to accept it. My emotions were wrong, and she gave me a look as if I had two heads. Clearly, she was the sane one, and my emotion was so insane that she refused even to address it. She was quite resentful of how I dared to look like that on Christmas morning but made it a point to move on quickly. After all, what was the point of wasting time on such complete nonsense? Looks like we've got a pretty ungrateful little girl on our hands. Maybe next year, she will have the right emotions! Some nerve….

"Better is a dinner of herbs where love is, than a fatted calf with hatred."
-Proverbs 15:17 [NKJV]

December 21st, 1986,
Merry Christmas to my Sweet Suzanne!

I hope you and your family can spend some time this season thinking about the humbling birth of the Savior of our world. I know you will, for sure! You were absolutely ravaging as Angel #3 in your Christmas pageant. Such an honor to be invited!

Merry Christmas to my Blue-Eyed Wonder.

Love,
Uncle Tommy

"He was born in an obscure village, the child of a peasant woman. He worked in a carpenter shop and was an itinerant preacher. He never wrote a book. He never held an office. He did none of the things one usually associates with greatness. Twenty centuries have come and gone and today, He is the central figure of the human race. All the armies that ever marched, all the navies that ever sailed, all the kings that ever reigned, put together, have not affected the life of those one earth as much as that one solitary life."
-James Francis

Chapter Eight
Hobbies

"Whoever causes one of these little ones who believe in me to fall away —it would be better for him if a heavy millstone were hung around his neck and he were drowned in the depths of the sea."
-Matthew 18:6 (NIV)

It was always difficult for me to keep hobbies growing up under the same roof as a terrifying narcissist. I had gifts and talents, and while Daddy tried his best to encourage me, he was very rarely home, so the majority of my home life was tragically spent with Mother. The book of Proverbs tells us as a man thinks in his heart, so is he. My life merely became a self-fulfilling prophecy to Mother's venomous words. Even though I was intelligent, funny, compassionate, and quite creative, I lived out the negatives. This is because even though they were lies, if people consistently hear something long enough, it doesn't really matter if it is true or not. Eventually, they will start to believe it and embrace it as truth. In my mind, I accepted the lie that I was a failure at everything.

Mother despised it when I began to collect specific things like glass Minnies and Mickeys and pigs. After all, I belonged to *her*. Who did I think I was, becoming my own unique person? Mother grinned and bore it until she noticed my deep love for music. It was the rhythm to which my heart beat.

My love for classic rock and roll, pop, and even classical music was taking it too far. Hearing the beautiful music coming from my room was like nails on a chalkboard for Mother, and day by day, she felt her power slowly fading away.

Finally, one day, Mother had decided she had had enough of this rebellious individuality. Every morning, I would set my alarm clock to music. It was the best way to wake up. After my shower, I would continue to listen to music as I got ready for the day. This is when she decided to attack.

Mother would scream up the stairs to turn down the music, typically followed by calling me "fat" or "whore" or some devilish combination of both terms. I weighed ninety seven pounds and had never had a boyfriend.

We've all heard the expression, "You catch more bees with honey than vinegar." Well, pardon me for not being eager to comply with her demands after being called names no woman (especially an innocent little girl) should ever be subjected to.

Consequently, I didn't listen.

This made Mother mad.

It's almost as if she knew I wouldn't listen and did it all on purpose so she could have my noncompliance to justify her next act.

Like a hiding lion about to pounce on its prey, Mother waited for just enough time to pass with the music still not being turned down. It was typically about one to two minutes.

Then, the attack began.

Driven by blinding rage, Mother began to scream and stormed up the steps. By this time, Mother had stripped all the locks off of every door in that home, so I was unable to protect myself or my room.

Every time I heard those footsteps, I knew the fate that awaited me. Mother slammed open the door and found me curled up and hiding in my closet. Sometimes, she went straight up to me and began physically beating me—punching, kicking, scratching, and even spitting in my face. Every now and then, I got a punch or two in myself, but she was much larger and always won.

After the physical beating, Mother would open up each of my dresser drawers and throw the contents about the room until, eventually, the entire dresser was empty and clothing was strewn everywhere.

Mother still wasn't done yet, though. It was time to strip this haughty sense of individuality her disrespectful daughter thought she had. She barged over to the bedside table where I kept my collectibles. One by one, each pig was picked up and shattered against the wall. The same was done with each of my Mickeys and Minnies. On later ransacks, Mother seemed to discover hidden or replaced treasures—shattering them each one by one until one day… they were all gone.

There was no point in replacing any more of them. Mother would find and destroy them on the next attack.

So, I finally stopped collecting pigs, Minnies, and Mickeys. I eventually came to a day where I said, "Well, I guess I don't collect pigs anymore."

Just like that, I was no longer a collector. I never again acquired a single pig, Minnie, or Mickey for the rest of my life.

Hunting Island Flashback: Still the Same Free Spirit

February 2nd, 1987,
My Sweet Suzanne,

I haven't heard from you since Christmas, and I could feel it was time for Good Ole Uncle Tommy to send some love your way! I did receive your collection of artwork and poetry, and it is displayed proudly upon my office bulletin board. It's always a good day whenever someone asks about the creator: it gives me a chance to talk about my wonderful, creative Suzanne! I hope you are doing well, my love, and never forget that I'm always thinking about you and praying for you.

All My Love and Affection,
Uncle Tommy

"No act of kindness, no matter how small, is ever wasted."
-Aesop, The Lion and the Mouse

Chapter Nine
Friendships

"A perverse [wo]man sows strife, and a whisperer separates the best of friends."
-Proverbs 16:28 [NKJV]

Up until my teenage years, when my friends and I finally figured out what Mother was doing, she managed to sabotage each and every one of my friendships as a little girl until I was left with none. Her go-to method was the same each time: She picked a fight with the friend's Mother. In a pinch, if the friend's mother was unavailable, she could always succeed by hounding either the father or a sibling.

I remember at one point, I had a cute poster hung on my wall with a dog snuggling with a kitten. The caption underneath the picture on the poster read, "Best friends are a special thing."

At one point, after she had succeeded in bulldozing each one of my friendships, she decided to walk into my room. Slowly, she turned her head and gazed at the friendship poster to the left of the door. I observed her silently studying the poster, and after some time, she glanced back at me.

With an eerie, calculating voice, she looked up from the poster and stated with her famous synthetic sympathetic tone, "But honey, do you even have any friends like that?"

I decided that a comment like that did not deserve the energy required for my response.

How she hated it when I acted like an adult better than she ever could!

After she left my room, I remember feeling angry because she was right, but I still couldn't quite figure out what she was doing to make me friendless. About a week passed, and in an air of defeat, I gave in and took the poster down. After all, she was right—thanks to her, it was true—I had no friends. Thanks, Ma.

Several weeks passed after the poster was removed when, sure enough, good ole Uncle Tommy's presence once again filled that violent household. His cards and messages always seemed to hold an uncanny resemblance to the reality of a particular trauma brought on by Mother.

A Vow of Friendship

I honor your path.
I drink from your well
I bring an unprotected heart to our meeting place.
I hold no cherished outcome.
I will not negotiate by withholding.
I am not subject to disappointment.

October 13th, 1988,
Suzy-Q!

My love, you are never going to believe what your crazy Uncle Tommy did! In August, my company made all of their employees attend a sales seminar at the large Atlanta Cobb EMC Arena. I don't know if you have ever been there, but it's not too difficult for somebody to get lost there. As it turned out, I, of course, had the wrong conference room number and ended up at a pre-party planning committee for a Kwanzaa social group.

Well, long story short, they served complimentary drinks and, as it turns out, I enjoyed the music, the culture, and the company.

You guessed it… I never made it to my original conference. Wayyy too many drinks, baby girl.

Well, allow me to be the first to officially wish you an early… HAPPY KWANZAA!!!

All My Love and More,
Uncle Tommy

A Poem for You

Suzy-Q,
Today when the sun wakes up,
And the dew drops in,
And the breeze whistles its song,
And the clouds dance on the wild blue yonder,
And the forest whispers its secrets,
And the mountains echo their wisdom,
And the rivers toll with laughter,
And the planet pirouettes in space,
Till the stars tip-toe softly
'Found the moon…
Today-
All Day-
Just know, it's ALL FOR YOU!

Chapter Ten
Pets

The issue of childhood pets was indeed a curious one. Brother and I grieved the loss of around ten (if not more) precious dogs throughout our childhood. The strange part was that we never had a dog. Allow me to explain.

About once or twice a year for five to six years, our family embarked on an exciting adventure to look for a puppy. Of course, there was always at least one that Brother and I fell head over heels in love with at each shelter we visited. To this day, I'm not entirely sure why Father even went. He knew he never had a say.

After all, Mother made all of the decisions…

With each visit, all of the signs looked good from Mother's standpoint. "Looks like a keeper! Would you just look at that face? That looks like a fella that could make us all very happy."

Though Mother would never personally touch or give the smallest embrace to any of the puppies, the forced smile on her face was at least comforting to Brother and me.

With each visit, like clockwork, the following pattern would occur:

We talked about a puppy for a few months

We visit some puppies

Brother, Father, and I fall in love with a puppy

Mother states, "Well, let's have a couple of weeks to talk about it at home with Dad!"

A couple of weeks go by and Brother and I follow up on the issue

Some inevitable excuse was made each time ("too much commitment," "maybe next time," "not the right puppy for us") and the case was closed until it was time for the next round

Looking back, I know Mother never intended to get a puppy. It was yet another one of her subtle torturous schemes, and it threw me off because she involved Brother, too.

There was, however, one round that I will never forget. It was the last and final round to the puppy torture that ensued upon Brother and me. This last time, she went for the throat; she was moving in for the kill.

I will never forget the last and final round of our puppy heartbreak because that time, somewhere in between steps five and six, she did something different. Mother went as far as to ask a neighbor for their extra doggie bed because we were looking to get a puppy.

When the bed arrived in our home, I remember placing it on the laundry room floor and feeling elated.

It's actually happening this time. We are finally getting a dog.

As expected, two more weeks passed between what I will now call step "five b" and "step six." Of course, after two weeks, Brother and I knew it was time to follow up on the dog that we were actually getting this time.

Something was different about this request. There was no suspicion—only hope. Mother had us where she wanted us. She filled us with hope and positioned us in a place to never expect the bombshell about to be dropped on both of us.

Forget about the rug being swept beneath our feet. This was an entire floor disappearing beneath our trusting feet, slamming us unexpectedly face down in life.

Her answer was eerie. Her answer was cold. To this day, her answer still gives me goosebumps. While I will never know what excuse she gave to Brother, I will never forget the chilling words she spoke to me.

"Honey, just think about all of the yelling that goes on in this house. That wouldn't be fair to a poor dog. It would be scared to death most of the time."

So, there it was.

To Mother's credit, she was right. An animal would be scared to death living in our violent home.

So what about the children who have no choice but to live there? That elephant was permanently implanted in the room and was never addressed, touched, or even acknowledged.

Just like that, the brutal round of "almost doggies" officially came to a close, leaving us to mourn the loss of pets we never even had.

But there was something uncanny about Mother's scheming on this last round. Even though she had given her final decree, for some sick reason, the empty dog bed stayed on the floor for months.

Why was it still there? Why am I even looking at this anymore? It was as if the pain from the memory of every "no" wasn't enough for my broken heart.

Months passed with it lying on the floor as a brutal reminder of everything (or nothing, depending on how you look at it). At this point, I cannot speak for Brother's emotions on the issue simply because she separated us and had a conversation at different times with us—unlike all the times before. A simple observation of his demeanor after our last and final cutthroat "step six" told me that, for some reason, he was disappointed but nowhere near the level of pure devastation I felt in my heart from the answer I was given.

I tried to avoid the room, but as it was the laundry room and the school supply room, there was no way around going in. I tried to ask Brother to go in there for me.

"Get it yourself. You have legs."

Even though, most of the times I went into that room, I refused to look at the empty bed, not looking at it didn't change the fact that it was there—a taunting reminder of it all. Even when I wasn't in that room, I was still aware of its presence to a certain degree.

Finally, one night, I had enough of the visual torture. It was trash night, and I knew nobody was going to put me out of this misery. When you grow up in an abusive home, you learn quickly to advocate for yourself. Nobody else will.

In an act of complete defeat and disgust, I took it upon myself to throw it out that night with the trash.

Mother saw what I did.

How she hated it when I saw through her plots.

"Now is your time of grief, but I will see you again and you will rejoice, and no one will take away your joy."
-James 16:22 [NIV]

January 12th 1989,

Happy New Year, Suzy-Q!

Your father tells me that your family has once again visited another animal shelter and came home without a pet. Why have there been so many "almosts" and still no furry critter to take home? I asked him to talk your mother into sealing the deal—why has nothing happened? It's important to have a pet—to have something to love. Sending unconditional love to you. Don't lose that sweet spirit.

I'll Love You as Long As Forever,
Uncle Tommy

Chapter Eleven

Nobody

In the fourth grade, I was given the assignment to memorize a poem, and if I could recite it to the class, I would receive extra credit on the upcoming math test. Now, as a child, I had lost count of how many books of poems (particularly Shel Silverstein poems) I had either read or checked out from the library. I will never forget that out of all the thick volumes, *Where the Sidewalk Ends* and *A Light in the Attic,* the poem I instantly chose was called "Nobody." Without a second thought, I stood up and recited the following poem to my entire fourth grade class:

"Nobody"

Nobody loves me,
Nobody cares,
Nobody picks me peaches and pears.
Nobody offers me candy and Cokes.
Nobody listens and laughs at my jokes.
Nobody helps when I get in a fight,
Nobody does my homework at night.
Nobody misses me,
Nobody cries,
Nobody thinks I'm a wonderful guy.
So if you ask me who's my best friend, in a whiz,
I'll stand up and tell you that "Nobody" is.
But yesterday night I got quite a scare,
I woke up and Nobody just wasn't there.
I called out and reached out for Nobody's hand,
In the darkness where Nobody usually stands.
Then I poked through the house, in each cranny and nook,
But I found somebody each place that I looked.
I searched till I'm tired, and now with the dawn,
There's no doubt about it-
Nobody's gone!

What a young age to be so sad, yet still hopeful that things would turn around.

I stood up to the class with my game face on and didn't miss a word. Something tells me that my teacher would have given me extra credit, regardless….

"How precious to me are your thoughts, God! How vast is the sum of them! Were I to count them, they would outnumber the grains of sand."
-Psalms 139:17 [NIV]

January 12th, 1990
Suzanne,

A poem for you.

Deep Love and Affection,
Good Ole Uncle Tommy

I Love You

The experience of Love is unilateral; It asks no response,
Nor does it demand the other to be deserving,
And every human being deserves Love.
It is not earned…one deserves it.
So, every human being offers us he opportunity of loving them.
The 'Loving' rewards, not the being loved.
Being made in the image of God, each of us deserves Love.
Our loving is our striving towards Godliness.
It is our privilege, not our duty.
Love has no rewards beyond the experience of it, nor does it require any.

'I Love You' means something very special and very concrete.
It means that I surround you with the feelings that allows you, perhaps
even requires you, to be everything you really are as a human being at that
moment. When my Love is fullest, you are most fully you.
You may be good, or bad, or both;
Or tender, or angry, or both…

But you are you,
Which is the very most I could ever ask, or expect.
And so, I experience you in all your beauty, and all your ugliness.
But you, not what I expect, or want, or what you feel you should be.

My Love of you enables you to be what you are.
'Love' shatters roles, and illuminates persons.
The acquired masks are discarded,
And we face each other as we are…
Really, and usually, wonderfully.

-Tom Malone

Hunting Island Flashback: Still the Same Free Spirit

Chapter Twelve

The "Yoke"

"Come to me, all you who are weary and burdened, and I will give you rest. Take my yoke upon you and learn from me, for I am gentle and humble in heart, and you will find rest for your souls. For my yoke is easy and my burden is light."
-Matthew 11:28-30 [NIV]

Jesus tells us to come to Him and He will give us rest. This verse has always captivated me because of his usage of the word "yoke." Many times throughout Tommy and Miriam's lives, they described Mother's influence over me as a "yoke." Even at a young age, something told me this was not the same "yoke" that Jesus refers to.

As I grew older, the word "yoke" continued to linger in my spirit, eventually leading me towards further research on what a yoke actually is as well as the difference between Mother's yoke and Jesus's yoke.

In Biblical times, a yoke was a heavy wooden harness placed on oxen and attached to the equipment the oxen pulled. As an adult still struggling with the long-term effects of child abuse, I knew Jesus's yoke was for me.

How were these two yokes different, then?

The yoke from Mother's child abuse was no different than the one on the oxen carrying overwhelming loads day in and day out; it could give only physical and mental persecution.

Although Jesus's yoke is an overwhelmingly better solution than Mother's yoke, Jesus's yoke is not all sunshine and roses—but it is undoubtedly worth the effort. Simply put, Jesus's yoke refers to the challenges of following him as a true disciple. As an adult, I learned that the responsibilities and effort required to live as a faithful Christian can still weigh us down.

So in what sense is Jesus's yoke easy?

Jesus's yoke is easy compared to the crushing yoke of an abused child who did not yet know our savior because, as Christians, we know we have a partner in life who shares the yoke of discipleship with us. Jesus's bigger shoulders carry the weight of the burdens of the Christian life and all the other things that can weigh down even the most devout Christians. If we are wise, we will allow Jesus's greater power to help us carry the everyday yoke of life. In doing so, we begin participating in life's responsibilities with a greater partner.

When I finally learned about Jesus, my beloved Godfather Tommy showed me Jesus's yoke.

Although scripture teaches us that the Christian life is not always easy, it also teaches us that Jesus's yoke gives rest to the burdened and weary.

What better way to show an abused little girl Jesus's rest than by taking her on a special trip? Tommy did that for me as much as possible. This time, he took Grandma Mimi and me to one of his favorite places in the world: the cultural district of New Orleans.

From as early as I can remember, my Godfather always spoke about the vibrant and lively tradition of New Orleans, from the festive Mardi Gras celebration to the famous foods of crawfish and beignets to the city's rich culture of music and art.

It was my first time flying on an airplane, and once again, I received little sleep the night before due to my pure excitement about the trip and the opportunity to get away and live in peace. Even if it was just for one week, I took it!

Like the vibrant artwork in the cards he sent me with each letter throughout my life, Tommy selected an artistic hotel for us to stay in. That was just Tommy's style. Nothing was ever mundane. Holiday Inn? The Marriott? Forget it! He rented out an entire art museum with an apartment suite on the top floor for us to stay in.

Why was I even surprised?

The museum was nothing short of stunning, and our top floor had a lovely balcony overlooking the heart of the French Quarter adjacent to Bourbon Street. I still didn't know much about Heaven at that age, but I was sure I was already there.

The trip was everything I dreamed of. We visited many museums, dined at eclectic restaurants, and participated in much of the daily New Orleans culture—including spontaneous dancing to music in the middle of the street.

Apparently, it didn't just happen in the musicals. It also happened in New Orleans.

Interestingly, my favorite part of the entire trip was not seeing any of the fancy places or even staying in the luxurious lodging. Don't get me wrong, I loved it all, but my fondest memory of the trip happened at an ordinary mall in downtown New Orleans.

Uncle Tommy, Mimi, and I had just finished lunch after checking out the local stores inside the strip mall when suddenly we reached two empty escalators that had been turned off, presumably for repairs. Of course, that's what the rest of the world saw. Uncle Tommy and I saw a spontaneous opportunity for a foot race.

It was Hunting Island all over again.

Without a word exchanged, Uncle Tommy and I looked at each other with mischievous grins. In a matter of seconds, Tommy ran around to the opposite escalator while yelling, "Don't you get a head start, young lady!"

He thought I needed a head start. Bless his heart.

Nevertheless, I obliged and waited until my beloved Godfather reached the other broken elevator.

Yellow tape? What yellow tape?

Uncle Tommy did the honors. "On your mark… Get set… GO!"

Instantly, we both embarked upon yet another spontaneous, free-spirited footrace which likely caught the attention of any bystander looking in that direction.

I was sweating it the first fourth of the journey. *What on Earth did this man eat for breakfast? I refuse to let a man twice my age beat me on an unplanned, illicit footrace down two broken elevators closed to the public.*

How Uncle Tommy and I went through life never spending a night in jail together is beyond me. Poor Mimi turned away in sheer humiliation and walked inside an adjacent store to pretend she knew neither of us. She had to do that often. She would be fine.

Alas, as Uncle Tommy and I neared the halfway point of our borderline illegal race on broken mall equipment, I took the lead. Never mind the fact that I was eight and he was forty-five, I was owning it because Uncle Tommy doesn't play—he was out to win, but not on my watch.

In triumphant glory, my feet hit the ground precisely five steps before my forty-five-year-old Godfather's did. Oh, the honor of sheer victory! I was sure to rub it in his face. Of course, he cited a technicality, as I may or may not have skipped a few steps. Still, I offered a quick rebuttal, citing a failure to provide specific rules to our unplanned, attention-gathering, socially frowned-upon pursuit.

At that point, we just looked at each other and began laughing to the point of joyful tears. Even during that moment, I knew it would be a memory forever kept fondly in my heart. Nevermind all the people around us looking at us as if we had just escaped an insane asylum. When you lived in my and Tommy's world, sometimes other people didn't exist. It was both a safe and exhilarating place to be.

In case you were wondering, yes, mall security kindly asked us to leave.

It was cool, we were finished shopping and hey, we didn't get arrested!

May 24th 1990,
My Dearest Suzanne,

May everything you love flow into your life.

Happy Birthday darlin' and at the appropriate hour… Happy Kwanzaa.

Uncle Tommy

Part Three
Fasten Your Seatbelts!

Chapter Thirteen
Entitlement

In the narcissistic family model of a narcissistic mother, the father is inevitably the enabler. In my case, my narcissistic Mother chose Brother to be the "golden child" and I was the "scapegoat." In essence, the golden child can do no wrong and is used to make the scapegoat feel worse about herself. As the only girl, I naturally became the scapegoat. I shifted through life as her porcelain doll into an adolescent who was naturally developing her sense of individuality. Since Mother was utterly insecure in her own identity—she certainly had no clue about who she was in Christ—she became increasingly more violent towards me as I got older and began developing my own personality.

Now that I have provided you with a brief rundown on narcissistic family models, it is time to discuss Brother; the "golden child."

As the name implies, he could do no wrong in Mother's eyes. Whatever Mother thought, felt, or discerned was what my father (the enabler) went along with. Mother had tragically made sure to decimate Father's sense of individuality, which prohibited any semblance of free thinking.

There is not much to state about Brother, only a few curious behaviors I observed growing up. Brother mistreated me simply because Mother (and, by extension, Father) taught him that he did not need to honor me.

Even as a child, the twisted sense of entitlement they showed to him made me sick to my stomach, and I knew that one day it would only work against him.

As a result of this unwarranted sense of entitlement gifted by Mother (and, by extension, Father), Brother began his youngest years simply not wanting to ever play with me. As a young girl, I remember this making me very sad and lonely. We were only two years apart in age. It would have been natural for us to spend some time together and for him to actually acknowledge my existence.

When we grew a bit older, Brother moved from never even looking at me to actively bullying me both at home and at school. Strangely, it was nice just to be acknowledged by him. He was a curious boy who encouraged his friends to bully me. Every now and then, one of his friends would decline because they knew it was so twisted. It was even more sick when Brother encouraged his friends at church to bully me. Perhaps even more disturbing was the fact that they all complied.

There was one summer when I was enrolled in dance camp. Mother had initially enrolled me for status, and she became quite enraged when she saw I was gifted in this area. As it turned out, Mother and Father worked when I needed to be driven there and picked up. Brother James had his license and refused to drive his little sister anywhere. As a result, Mother and Father actually paid Brother to drive and pick me up from dance camp that week.

They had to pay him to do what older siblings are naturally expected to do for younger siblings.

Gross.

I've mentioned the phenomenon of self-fulfilling prophecies. While Mother couldn't bring herself to say or show him genuine love (only favoritism), the lack of verbal abuse and constant comparison to his "good for nothing" little sister gave him just enough freedom to excel in school. This was Mother's plan. His sense of individuality was still stifled, but he needed to make good grades so that I could see how stupid I was in comparison.

I will never forget the lavish, ornate, tall mahogany wood desk they bought for Brother. Meanwhile, I received a thrift store white small desk with the paint chipped off. After all, Mother couldn't make it too obvious what she was doing. I remember never having any room for everything on that desk, and by extension, I didn't have an established place to do my schoolwork. With Brother's expensive royalty desk, he was all set for success. As for me, I roamed for places around the house to do my subpar work. It never really mattered, though. I was a C student at best in public school. When you are told you are stupid, you act that way, whether it is true or not.

As I look back upon those days, I realize the only person free enough to express the slightest semblance of individuality was Brother. Yet, ironically, he stayed bound by the system into adulthood and never experienced the freedom of knowing the truth. Back then, I would have done almost anything to have been accepted by Mother as he was. Now, I see my role in the system as a hidden gift. You see, because I was treated so horrifically, I got the real answers to what was going on in that family. The favoritism Brother received growing up would become a future prison for him. Not only did he never learn the truth about what was happening in our family, but he grew into a lonely, bitter insurance agent who never married. Brother never came close to marrying simply because the only way he knew how to treat women was based on a lifetime of observing Mother horrifically abuse his sister.

You can imagine how well that went over with the ladies.

To this day, as a grown man without a family of his own, all he has is my aging parents. When they leave this world, I hope he comes to know Jesus. I would let him back into my life. If Jesus forgave me of all my sins, who am I to hold a grudge against Brother who—in my opinion—honestly did not know any better? I think Brother has the potential to be a wonderful person, but I likely won't see this until he is officially on his own in the world.

"If you show favoritism, you sin and are convicted by the law as the lawbreakers."
-James 2:9 [NIV]

August 12th 1990,
My Darling Suzanne,

I saw this artwork on a greeting card at the annual art fest near my condo downtown and I thought of you, because you could "lasso the moon." I know you are growing up so fast now, but as your adoring Godfather, in my eyes, I will always see you at such a young age.

You and I are kindred spirits, my dear. Your grandmother Mimi knew this all too well throughout her lifetime. I know she is beaming down at you right now with pride!

Never lose that creative spirit. Keep writing! I know one day you will do wonderful things!!!

I Love You Always and in All Ways,
Uncle Tommy

Chapter Fourteen

The Lesser Elizabeth

Before I was born, I had a sister who died. She was a sinless soul, having lived only seven days, and the date of her death was July 7th, 1977.

Her name was Christine Elizabeth.

The Bible frequently refers to the number seven as perfection and completion. It is often a holy, prophetic Biblical number—God-breathed, in a sense.

So, let's summarize: Christine Elizabeth lived on this earth for seven days. The date of her death was July 7th, 1977. Everything about her was pure, Godly perfection.

When I was born, my parents gave me the name Suzanne Elizabeth.

Elizabeth.

We shared two-thirds of the same name. Any time I did something wrong or Mother ridiculed me, it was impossible for me not to feel compared to my deceased sister, who literally never sinned. It felt like I was dishonoring her name.

I was the lesser Elizabeth.

I could never live up to Christine Elizabeth. It would have been like living up to Christ Himself. It was a shadow constantly lingering over me—one I never asked for but got anyway.

Around age nine, I was being a kid and sneaking around in Brother's room, and what I found hidden in his desk drawer would change the trajectory of my life for over 40 years.

Eerily tucked away in his bottom right desk drawer, I discovered a letter he wrote titled:

"Why I Wish Christine Had Lived and Suzanne Were Never Born."

He wrote this letter by hand with a pencil. It was three pages, front and back. He even drew pictures and colored them with crayons to prove his points.

Perhaps the most eerie fact about this situation is that it was secretly hidden in his ornate mahogany desk. To me, it would be one thing (and I would almost expect it) if he had written it and spitefully shoved it in my face.

But, no… this was tucked away in a corner of his bedroom desk. He did not want anyone to read it.

To me, that's probably the most disturbing part of the whole ordeal.

After reading the letter, I took it and kept it in my room. After a few days, I gathered enough courage to confront Mother and Father about it.

When I finally showed Mother and Father the letter, they neither said nor did a thing.

In my mind, Mother and Father confirmed it all. Suzanne Elizabeth, as the letter stated, was a replacement for Christine Elizabeth.

I wasn't me. I was a replacement for my dead sister.

As I grew into adulthood, I naturally started having questions about Mother and did some ancestral research on my lineage. I was chilled to the bone to learn that my name was not the only dead baby replacement name in that family.

When Mother was five years old, she had a younger brother who died at the age of three in his crib. When my brother was born after Christine's death, he was given the name James, which seemed natural as James was one of Father's good friends at the time.

I will give you three guesses as to what Mother's dead baby brother's name also was.

To this day, I'm convinced she would have straight-up named me Christine Elizabeth all over again at my birth if it had not been so apparent to the public eye.

The backstory—the truth—behind Brother's birth name chills me even more. Nobody caught on.

I Am NOT a Replacement!

I Am a Child of God

"Blameless and innocent child of God without blemish in the midst of a crooked and twisted generation…I shine as a light in the world."
-Philippians 2:14-15 [NIV]

I Am Saved

"God showed his love for us in that while we were still sinners, Christ died for us."
-Romans 5:8 [NIV]

I Am Wonderfully Made

"I praise you, for I am fearfully and wonderfully made."
-Psalm 139:14 [NIV]

I Am Cared For

"Casting all your anxieties on him, because he cares for you."
-1 Peter 5:7 [NIV]

I Have Perfect Peace

"You will keep him in perfect peace whose mind is stayed on you, because he trusts in you."
-Isaiah 26:3 [NIV]

I Am Protected

"For God—his way is perfect; the word of the LORD proves true; he is a shield for all those who take Refuge in him."
-Psalm 18:30 [NIV]

November 12th, 1991,
Suzanne, My Beloved,

In all of the universe… there is ONLY ONE YOU!!! Miss and love you deeply,

Uncle Tommy

"I would rather be ashes than dust,
I would rather my spark should
Burn out in a brilliant blaze
Than it should be stifled in dry-rot.
I would rather be a superb meteor,
Every atom of me in magnificent glow,
Than a sleepy & permanent planet.
Man's chief purpose is to Live,
Not to Exist.
I shall not waste my days trying to prolong them.
I shall use my time, I shall Live!"

-Jack London

Chapter Fifteen

Home Cuffs

The older I got, the more my home life felt like an R-rated movie where I was the star. As it turns out, being repeatedly called a "visitor" in my own home did not make me feel so "at home."

"This is not your home. You are just a visitor."

Destruction of property—especially special things—became something that I began to expect in that house.

When Disney's *Aladdin* came out, I remember Mother bought me an *Aladdin* puzzle that was so big it took up the entire dining room table. It wasn't a cheap puzzle, and she bought it for *me*. She must *really* love me to spend this much!

It took me weeks, but my big moment finally came. I placed the last piece onto a magical tapestry of Jasmine and Aladdin riding on the magic carpet. I will never forget that feeling. It was the first time I completed an entire giant puzzle alone.

Mother even let me keep the finished version on the dining room table until something happened.

Before I knew it, I found myself amidst yet another domestic war zone. Dishes were being thrown into the air, crashing relentlessly against the walls. A bagel with cream cheese was thrown at my head. I must have had the reflexes of Mary Lou Renton back then because I ducked just in time, causing the creamed cheese bagel to stick to the wall behind me.

Some things were almost funny, were they not so tragic.

It didn't take a rocket scientist to conclude that it was time to leave the kitchen for my safety. Quickly, I moved to the dining room to protect my masterpiece puzzle.

That's the problem with Mother, though. It seemed she was always one step ahead of me during the attacks. Without skipping a beat, Mother barged into the living room.

The second she entered, I knew it was all over.

Mother started with the corner pieces, grabbing chunks of the puzzle and mercilessly throwing them about the room in any direction she saw fit.

At some point, I imagine things weren't moving fast enough for Mother. Her following action would become an image ingrained in my mind for the rest of my life.

With a single motion, Mother held both arms out and carefully moved the remaining puzzle pieces in the opposite direction. In a single, calculated swoop, Mother destroyed my remaining hopes of repairing my puzzle.

I should have known there was no hope when Mother entered the room.

To this day, I'm still unsure as to why I treasured that puzzle so dearly. Perhaps because it captured the movie scene where Princess Jasmine and Aladdin sing about *"A Whole New World."*

They were singing about the thing I desperately wanted but, no matter how hard I tried, could never attain: A whole new world.

It was only a matter of time until the night before the first day of my sophomore year was upon me. I always had to be super careful on any night before a big day—it was Mother's favorite time to attack.

Despite my best attempts to please Mother, she picked a fight with me anyway. After all, it was almost my first day of school as a sophomore. She would be a fool to miss this opportunity to jeopardize my day.

Like all typical fights, it started with yelling and name-calling. This time, there were punches on the main level stairs. She caught me trying to escape. She spit in my face. I spat right back.

Lucky for me, all I had to do was to escape her grip and run into the upstairs bathroom. Although Mother had intentionally stripped the locks of all the doors in that house, I found a loophole. In times of the most extreme danger, it was ideal for me to be near the upstairs bathroom because there was a drawer adjacent to the door inside the bathroom. All I had to do was open it far enough and it blocked the door from opening up entirely. Nobody could hurt me at that moment.

I did just that.

I was safe. Even though I saw her ferocious face yelling every name in the book at me in the space between the cracked door and the drawer that kept it closed, I had never felt safer than when I was inside that bathroom and Mother was on the outside, unable to get in.

I knew she would be out there for a while, so at least I could access a toilet. Speaking of the toilet, it made for a nice seat for me just to rest and kill time during her typical outside-the-door tantrums.

Everything was going well for me on my end until I gazed upon the side of the shower. In a moment of horror, I realized that I had forgotten to bring the bottle of shampoo that Mother bought for me to use in the morning upstairs.

It's almost as if she and I were on the same wavelength because as soon as I realized she had access to something I needed for that next day, everything got quiet.

No. Please no. I have to wash and fix my hair for the first day of school. God, let her forget. Let her go downstairs for a quick breather in between rages. Don't let her do what I think she's about to do.

That's the thing about abuse. Typically, the one being abused becomes an expert at predicting how the abuser will behave in certain situations. I did, anyway.

No more than two minutes had passed until I heard the familiar sound of the terrifying barge noise made as Mother stomped up the steps.

I called it; she had the shampoo in her hands. It's funny how she didn't even bother to grab the conditioner because she knew I could go without conditioner, but I had to have shampoo, or else my hair would become a total grease machine.

In an air of desperation, I was brave enough to even stick my head out of the cracked open door, risking a myriad of head and face injuries.

"Mom, I'm so sorry—please... I need my shampoo for tomorrow. I'll do whatever; you can scream in my face for as long as you want. Mom, I'll clean the whole house. Please, mom, what do you need me to do?"

But it was useless; she had me exactly where she wanted me.

"So, you need this shampoo, you say?"

There was no use in answering her. It was over.

To my horror, I watched a grown woman pour an entire bottle of Herbal Essence shampoo over the whole carpet in the upstairs hallway. I even remember hearing the noise it made at the very end upon squeezing the final remnants out of an empty bottle.

She knew I would do whatever it took at age fourteen to scrape up some of that shampoo, so she took the bottle with her before leaving the scene of the attack. Before leaving, she stuck her frightful face in the opening between the cracked door and the open drawer. I yelped in surprise and fear.

She turned around and opened the medicine closet across the hall from the bathroom door. I heard two separate loud thumps of things thrown at the door. She had hurled a can of carpet cleaner and a cleaning brush at the bathroom door.

"NOW CLEAN UP THIS MESS BEFORE I DO SOMETHING WORSE!"

"Fine, but if I clean up your mess, you can't touch me when I'm out here."

It's amazing—really more pathetic—how I thought she would ever play fair with anything.

There was no response. I had no guarantee she wouldn't hurt me when I came out of the safety of the bathroom.

It was perhaps one of the bravest, possibly stupidest, moments of my life, but I closed the inside drawer, came out of the protection of the bathroom, knelt on the floor, and began cleaning up the astronomical mess.

I made sure not to veer too far from the bathroom door in case she decided to visit me with a surprise attack as I knelt on the floor cleaning up her mess.

I heard nothing. That was disturbing. Every few minutes, I walked to the end of the hall and peeked down the stairs to see if I could see or hear her anywhere. She was nowhere to be found. Maybe if I cleaned it up in enough time, she could go back to the store and buy more. It was 10 P.M., though, and it wasn't looking good.

Just moments before I finished cleaning up the wreckage upstairs, Mother's voice emerged from the bottom of the steps. It startled me so much that it made the hairs on my arms and back of my neck stand straight up.

"Little bitch—where are you?" I knew she was calling out to me.

I peeked my head out from the side of the upstairs wall, and before I could tell her I was finished, she looked me straight in the eye and said the most bone-chilling words I had ever heard in my entire life.

"Suzanne, you little whore, I almost forgot to tell you—if tonight, you do decide to kill yourself, please do me a favor and do it on the hardwood floor. There's no way I could get that much blood out of the carpet."

Now she cares about the carpet.

Undoubtedly, my high school years were by far the most violent years with Mother in that house.

Even though the intensity of abuse increased, I never stopped being her porcelain doll. After all, in Mother's eyes, everything about me—the way I looked, what I wore, how I acted—was always a direct reflection of her.

There were two different types of mornings while getting ready for high school in that house: the non-attack mornings and the attack mornings.

On the former, I rode the school bus; on the latter, Mother drove me. Mother drove me not because she wanted to comfort me, of course, but because she had figured out that a combination of her special concealer plus the air conditioner on high speed towards my face during the drive to school was just enough to make it appear like I had not been crying.

After all, she could never let anybody know the *truth* about who she was and what she was doing. That would annihilate the image she had worked so hard to fabricate.

She might have fooled the authorities, the social workers, and the teachers at school, but at a certain point, there's only so much you can hide from your neighbors.

Indeed, the neighbors were starting to get suspicious. Could it be all the crying, yelling, and screaming? My friend, who lived next door during that time, who heard me?

One night changed it all for the neighbors who lived the nearest to that house—the ones who were "on the fence," as it were.

Earlier that evening, before dusk, I had discovered my diary opened up right on Mother's nightstand. I knew for a few days that it was missing, and of course, I knew Mother was the culprit.

Mother must have been slipping, though. She was usually so careful and crafty—what was she thinking, leaving it out in plain sight like this?

At that moment, I realized I could take it back and hide it somewhere else, but the sad reality was that I knew it was only a matter of time before Mother would find the new location and take it back. Unlike most girls who kept a diary, I was deprived of the cathartic, freeing experience associated with keeping a diary because I knew Mother would find and read it.

So, just like that, I decided I no longer wanted a diary. At that moment, I knew what I had to do. I had to destroy it. Unlike Brother, who was known to secretly burn things for no reason in our basement, I was smart enough to know that Smokey's friends don't start fires.

`I had to find a different way.

So, I decided to take the diary and walk outside to the edge of our property, rip it into pieces, and throw it in the sewer by our house.

It's important to remember that this all happened before dusk.

Mother saw me.

By now, you're probably expecting me to say she just beat me up or destroyed my room.

No.

To this day, I laugh at how Mother handled this because it was the beginning of the end for her (as far as her precious reputation went).

Indeed, she went too far, and her actions only hurt her in the long run.

As soon as I walked back inside, Mother stormed past me, opened the front door, and trudged up the driveway to the sewer where I had ripped up and thrown the pieces of my diary.

I was watching it all from the dining room window, and I almost felt like I needed some popcorn and candy for this level of entertainment.

Mother arrived at the sewer which held the pieces of my destroyed diary.

I knew she had taken her "crazy" to a new level.

What I was about to see, to this day, still makes me laugh, as I know the neighbors knew for sure she was completely insane.

At that moment, she knelt, picked up the rusted covering of the sewer, and—like a Teenage Mutant Ninja Turtle—she climbed down the steps to the bottom of the sewer and began retrieving the ripped pieces of my diary on the bottom of the Cobb County public sewer.

At this point, I didn't even care if she did retrieve it all and taped it back together (she never got everything, but she did get a bunch and attempted to repair her daughter's ripped diary). I knew she had gone too far, and people were watching her from inside their homes along with me.

Mother was outside for hours; eventually, I got bored of watching her dig her own social grave and ended up doing something else.

That year marked the first time she stopped receiving Christmas cards and invitations to social events from our neighbors. I knew she was completely losing her mind in her pursuit to ruin my life.

I sure hope it was all worth it for her.

"In everything… set… an example by doing what is good. In your teaching show integrity, seriousness, and soundness of speech that cannot be condemned…"
-Titus 2:7-8

March 9th, 1991,

My Dearest Suzanne,

Hello my sweetness! I haven't heard from you or your father since we were all together for New Years, so I thought I would send some love your way…

Is everything okay at home? You know you can tell me anything baby girl—no matter what. Please remember that and know no matter what the case, for as long as forever, I will be here for you.

Keep nourishing that creative spirit! I can't wait for your next short story or poem.

Till we meet again.

Affectionately Yours,
Uncle Tommy

P.S.- I've been putting a lot of thought into it, and… I just don't think "being an adult" is gonna work for me!

Chapter Sixteen

The Bath

It was during those high school days when I received the worst of Mother's most violent abuse that I experienced the most horrifying night of my entire life.

We had just finished eating dinner when my best friend, Darcy, called on the landline.

Mother deeply resented that I caught on to how she was sabotaging my friendships in my younger years. Therefore, she despised every friend I had.

With Mother's cunning ability to eavesdrop, talking openly with Darcy over the phone proved extremely difficult. Typically, it was wisest to wait until the next day to talk.

For whatever reason, I must have been feeling foolishly brave that particular evening. I decided to whisper to Darcy every single detail of the abuse I experienced from the minute I got home from school to then.

About fifteen minutes went by until I suddenly felt as if we were being listened to.

"Hey Darcy, give me just a minute; I need to ask my Dad a question down here."

Only, I sprinted up the stairs to the first bedroom on the left: Mother's room.

There she was, sprawled out on the bed with the phone retriever to her ear as she held a pencil and a notebook in her hand.

When I opened the door and she saw that I had caught her, she unplugged the phone jack from the wall and immediately cut the connection.

"You think you're smart spying on me like that, you little bitch? I know all the things you said to your street-hook friend Darcy."

I knew I was in physical danger; I didn't waste any time talking—I just made a run for it. By the grace of God, she still had not thought to remove the lower bathroom drawer, and it was my only chance for physical safety.

Some nights, I made it. Some nights, I didn't.

On this night, I was simply out of luck. You see, I was fast enough to make it to the inside of the bathroom. The only problem was that I was shaking like a leaf and a hairbrush was blocking the top of the inside drawer. When you performed the drawer maneuver, every second counted.

The drawer wouldn't open. I was out of luck and out of time.

She grabbed my hair, holding my head in place, and forcefully slapped me several times across the face. She loved kicking my shins after she finished with my face.

This time, once she was finished with my body, she tried something new.

She looked me straight in the eye and, with a devilish smirk on her face, said, *"I think it's time you cool your jets."*

With that, she turned the shower head on and adjusted the water to icy cold. Within seconds, she violently shoved me into the tub, and I fell inside with all of my clothes (including my socks and shoes) still on.

She stood by the tub with her arms crossed, keeping guard to ensure I would not escape. Sometimes, I was tough; sometimes, I fought back. This time, she got me. All I did was wail helplessly as I continued to get soaked from head to toe in sub-zero water temperatures.

After about five minutes of Mother's torture chamber, she took a new approach because she knew it was getting late.

Mother switched the water source from the shower head to the bathtub faucet and closed the drain.

Immediately, the tub began to fill up with water, which was still ice cold.

"What are you doing you psycho?!" I yelled.

Mother didn't answer until the water reached the three-fourths mark.

"You're not done cooling your jets, Suzanne. The decent people in this house are going to sleep in beds tonight. You're going to sleep right here and cool your jets."

She started to leave the room but turned around once again. It was as if Satan himself were speaking directly to me when she made her last comment: *"And mark my words, Suzanne, if you try and sneak out of this tub, get dried off, and go to sleep in your bed, I promise you, you will wake up in Hell."*

Perhaps the most heartbreaking aspect of this all was that *I actually believed her.*

The next hour of my life was a complete blur. I knew time was passing, but I seemed to be stuck. I began to lose the concept of time, and all I did was alternate moving certain body parts out of the tub so that at least one part of my body was not submerged in the freezing temperatures at any given time.

I knew my body temperature was dropping, and I knew that one day I was going to die—but it wasn't going to be tonight.

I entered into fight or flight mode to save my life.

By now, she was likely asleep, so I carefully and slowly exited the tub and stayed as silent as humanly possible.

The doors were old, so my best chance of a silent open was to grip the handle and quickly bust it open.

It worked. It made not one sound. All the lights were off, and everybody was asleep.

Now, it was time for the linen closet. I prayed that Mother had not taken all of the towels out and hidden them somewhere. Although it was only a few feet away, moving from the bathroom door to the linen closet required masterful skill. I had grown to memorize the spots on the floor that creaked.

Much to my chagrin, the space between the bathroom door and the linen closet was a complete landmine of floor creaks. *Step on that, and I am toast.*

I quietly tiptoed to the left and took the long way around. It took a few steps to the left before I had cleared the "creak zone," so I began tiptoeing straight toward the door. Once I reached the wall, I had to tiptoe back to the right a few steps, and I made it creak-free to the linen closet door.

Once I reached the linen closet door, the same door technique as before was required for a quiet, successful opening.

The knob slowly but firmly turned in my hand. I closed my eyes, held my breath, and yanked open the door—no sound was made.

God was watching out for me. Mother had forgotten to pilfer all the towels and linens.

I'm not going to die! I'm not going to die!

Quickly and quietly, I grabbed two towels: one for my hair and one for my body. For me to move past the linen closet entrance without stepping on the landmine floor creak between the bathroom and the linen closet, I had to turn the knob and quickly shut the linen closet door. I was three for three with my seamless door maneuvers.

The journey from the linen closet to my bedroom had only one landmine floor creak to avoid. I successfully tiptoed around it and made it safely to my bedroom. I didn't even bother closing my bedroom door. If it wasn't necessary, it wasn't worth the risk of making a sound.

Once I dried off and changed into some dry clothes, I pulled back the comforter of my warm bed and crawled inside.

As I lay in my bed staring at the glow-in-the-dark stars I had placed on my ceiling at age seven, I found that I could not fall asleep.

Mother's words stuck with me: *"If you sleep in your bed tonight, you will wake up in Hell."*

"...Sleep in your bed tonight and wake up in Hell."

"Wake. Up. In. Hell."

At that age, I was still completely unaware of God's love and mercy for me. Furthermore, even though it did not make a lick of sense, I believed her.

In those days, there was probably only one thing scarier than Mother, and that was Hell. I didn't want to go to Hell. I was sweet. I had a cute little laugh. I was creative. I was funny. I would not fit in.

The idea terrified me and crippled my ability even to shut my eyes for a moment.

Time, once again, became a relative concept. I had no clue what the hour was, but the moment I heard the first morning bird sing in the darkness, I shot out of my warm bed like a bolt of lightning, put my cold, wet clothes back on, and performed my careful landmine-creak-avoiding maneuver to quietly make my way back to the scene of the crime.

The water in the tub was stagnant and cold. I did not bother to drain it, as something told me I would return here before sunrise.

I had already saved my life once that night; I refused to jeopardize it all over again by getting back in that tub. My body temperature was already dropping again from the icy, wet clothes. I planned to have a seat on the toilet and wait for the sound of Mother's footsteps.

Her footsteps were profoundly different from everybody else's. The sound of them was ingrained in my memory bank, for better or for worse.

Once I heard Mother approaching the bathroom, I would quickly and quietly jump back in the tub to make it seem like I had never moved.

Time was, once again, a relative concept, and I fell back into a daze. I had no idea what the hour was, but I could see from the bathroom window that it was dawn, so I knew Mother would be up soon.

Exhausted, I placed my arm on the nearby sink and laid my head down. Ironically, the scene of the crime was the only place where I felt safe enough to close my eyes. This was the first time I had ever stayed awake all night.

Although I closed my eyes for a few moments, I always caught myself and shot back up the moment I felt myself drifting into sleep. I still had no clue what time it was, but I began to hear Brother in his bedroom, so I needed to be ready.

Suddenly, it happened. Mother's door opened, and I made a beeline to the tub and sat back in. My splash did not worry me so much, as she never told me I couldn't make any noise while in the tub: I just had to stay there all night.

A numbing, icy sensation again spread across every inch of my frozen body.

It took only seconds to realize those were not Mother's footsteps. They were Father's, and he was going downstairs to make coffee.

I wasn't going to waste a single minute in that torture chamber if I didn't have to, so I got back out and resumed my former position on the toilet. I was ready for her rottenness to emerge and have this entire nightmare over with. I prayed to a God I did not know. I asked him to please let her come out of that room and put me out of my misery.

That God I did not know answered me. Within seconds after saying "amen," Mother's footsteps emerged from her bedroom into the hall.

It was go-time. As silently as I could, I bolted back into the bathtub. I waited for Mother's horrifying face to appear in the crack of the opened bathroom door.

To my surprise, Mother's footsteps were moving further away from me. She went straight downstairs without even bothering to check up on the status of her torture chamber victim. Why did she go straight downstairs?

For some reason, I felt safe enough to exit the bath, but I did not drain the water just to be sure. With Mother and Father downstairs, I decided it was safe to perform the quiet door-opening maneuver for the linen closet. I would wait until Brother went downstairs to get more towels from the linen closet. It wasn't worth risking the time and noise to return to my bedroom and retrieve the original towels I used that night.

Moments later, Brother opened his door and followed the crowd to the downstairs kitchen. I waited for him to walk the entire flight of steps and exit the entryway until I quietly opened the bathroom door. For some reason, I didn't bother avoiding the landmine floor creaks this time. I just walked straight to the linen closet and grabbed two fresh, beautiful towels.

I returned to the bathroom and decided I could not bear having these wet clothes on for another moment, so I took them off and dried myself with a towel.

I felt the same relief I experienced earlier that night when I first changed clothes and climbed into my warm bed. My body temperature was once again rising. Somehow, I still knew not to be cocky enough to go back into my bedroom, so I just sat there once again on the toilet and waited for someone to summon me.

It's almost as if Mother enjoyed this final stage of torture by continuing to avoid speaking with me. Without any interaction, for all I knew, she expected the torture to continue. In my mind, I needed her word, her confirmation that her daughter was no longer her prisoner for the time being. Mother knew I was waiting to hear from her.

It was a Saturday morning, and I could tell the three people who slept in beds last night were preparing breakfast. I started to count all the small tiles on the bathroom floor, even though I already knew there were fifty-seven total. This wasn't my first rodeo. With the bathroom drawer that kept the door from opening, I spent more time in that room than any other room in the house. It was the only place where I was truly safe.

I was on tile number twenty-three when I must have jumped several feet as I heard Brother shouting: *"Suzanne, come down for breakfast!"*

Breakfast? First, she nearly kills me, then, she offers me breakfast. It made no sense, but I wasn't about to disobey orders.

"I'll be right there!" I replied with a tone of hope and relief. Quickly, I walked to my bedroom, threw on the dry clothes I tried to sleep in, and walked down the stairs to join the rest for breakfast.

Mother made eggs and cream of wheat. I grabbed my plate and sat down without a word.

"Would you like milk or orange juice, sweetie?"

Suddenly, my torturer was nice. I wasn't about to push her back into psycho mode, though. "I'll have orange juice, thank you," I replied sweetly.

Within moments, the four of us were all sitting at the breakfast table, having breakfast together like the Brady Bunch. Not a word was spoken, though. I wasn't sure who was going to be the one to break the ice, but all I knew was that it wasn't going to be me.

I reached a point where I was convinced we would eat the entire meal silently until I saw Mother stop eating and blankly gaze out the window.

It's going to speak!

However, Mother did not address the family right away. It's almost as if she purposely paused for an added dramatic effect. Two unnecessary minutes passed, with her looking out the window until she decided to activate her vocal cords.

In a casual voice, as if discussing the weather or plans for the day, Mother addressed the family and stated, *"Last night, before I fell asleep, I want you to know that I saw an image of a green figure hovering over me in the bed. I felt my body moving upwards towards it, and then my body went back down to the bed, and it went away."*

I was glad to hear she got a good night's rest.

"Do not provoke your children to anger, do not exasperate them to the point of resentment with demands that are trivial or unreasonable or humiliating or abusive; nor by showing favoritism or indifference to any of them but bring them up tenderly with loving kindness in the discipline and instruction of the Lord."
-Ephesians 6:4 (AMP)

February 3rd 1993,
My Dearest Suzanne,

No special occasion, just saw this magical card and wanted to say I hope
you have an enchanted day!

"It's not what you look at that matters, it's what you see!"

I Love You,
Uncle Tommy

Chapter Seventeen

The Runaway

"For it is better to live on a corner of a roof than share a house with a contentious woman."
-Proverbs 21:19 [NIV]

"Look and see there is no one at my right hand; no one is concerned for me. I have no refuge; no one cares for my life. I cry to you, LORD, I say, 'You are my refuge, my portion in the land of the living.'"
-Psalm 142:4-5 [NIV]

Somewhere between eleven and twelve, I decided enough was enough. The next time I was faced head-on with one of Mother's terror attacks, the solution was simple: I would leave.

Where would I go? I don't know. How long would I stay? No clue.

Though I was not yet a teenager, I knew I had met my threshold when it came to Mother.

Sometimes, when I was lucky, I would have enough time to grab a pair of shoes before fleeing to safety. Other times, the fight-or-flight response kicked in and I was forced to sprint off either barefoot or wearing socks.

As a young runaway, I saw the nearby housing community under construction as an opportunity for me. The lavish, semi-finished homes provided a much-needed sanctuary for me amidst each episode of abuse.

I preferred it when Mother abused me when it was still daylight outside because most of the empty homes remained unlocked. I must have spent hours just sitting on the newly carpeted floors of these homes as I peered out the window, wondering what it would be like to have a normal, loving mother. Typically, I could stay in any home for between 30 minutes to several hours before a worker came in or a realtor brought a family inside. Whenever that happened, I would sit up and casually walk around the house for a bit as if I were in the market for a new home at age twelve. After a few minutes of my act, I would casually and politely exit the house, giving a warm smile and a "hello" to anyone I came across. After all, I couldn't let them know a vagrant was using the property to protect herself. I couldn't blow my cover.

Once I left a house, I would casually walk the rest of the neighborhood until I came across the next available shelter. This was my procedure for daytime attacks.

Nighttime attacks weren't so easy. In the event of a typical terror attack from Mother, I would not come back to the house for a minimum of two hours. Of course, this posed a problem when she attacked right before bedtime, because all the homes under construction were locked up for the evening and I needed a place to sleep.

Even though I knew I would most likely not gain access to any of the houses in the neighboring community at nighttime, I still ran to them during each nighttime attack anyway.

In most cases, I was too scared to pull the door handle of these homes at night because I didn't want some alarm to go off. It's funny how I always went to this community even though I knew I would never find shelter there.

It was far enough from that house to feel safe, and I was comforted by the memories of peace and protection associated with my daytime adventures there.

Unlike my daytime escapades, I was careful to not be seen during my nighttime visits. This mainly meant walking in the yards, away from streetlights or the sidewalk.

After a certain time (like a dog gone astray), I would find a backyard, lie on the ground, and cover my body with leaves. Even though I stayed in that position for hours, I never fell asleep. How could I? Most nights, I did this for several hours or until dawn. I always made sure that enough time had passed before I came back to the house after running away. They never got angry at me for running away. Never once was I looked for. Running away was just about the only thing I did not get in trouble for those days.

When I say "run away," I often literally ran away with Mother's husky body trailing behind, trying to catch me. Running away became a way of life for me—an escape. After all, what other choice did I have? It's not like I could go to the police and tell them the truth. Mother had made sure to place what is called "system fear" into me for as long as I could remember.

Essentially, system fear is a method of manipulation an abuser uses to try and keep their victim from going to the authorities based on the thought that "the system is so much worse."

It's sad to say that this is the truth, but there have been so many times when I wondered how my life would have turned out if I had called her bluff and reported her anyway.

I wish I had had the courage to weep in my Godfather's arms and tell him everything. Tommy would have taken me in a heartbeat. Mother would have fought quite the fight, but Tommy wouldn't back down. To him, I was worth it.

Alas, the fear of Mother trumped any semblance of courage in telling my Godfather the truth.

 The fact is, Tommy already knew something was up with Mother. He had never liked her from the moment he met her. Although my beloved Godfather was never aware of the extent of Mother's abuse, he and Mimi still knew things weren't right.

As it turns out, Mother had been on to Tommy and Mimi for a long time. While Mother's a lot of things, she was nobody's idiot. Although Tommy was my legal Godfather, I lost count of the times Mother would strangely tell me, *"If anything ever happened to your father and me, you would stay with your Aunt Carol."*

What a strange thing to say once, let alone repeatedly, to me throughout my life. Aunt Carol? Her son, my first cousin, had been sexually molesting me for as long as I could remember. Everybody knew, too. I never had the courage to tell Tommy about the sexual abuse, though. He's the only person who would have done something.

To recap, Mother ensured that plan B (Tommy) wasn't an option for me. After all, she knew he would raise and love me right—she couldn't have that. Mother manipulatively secured a similarly abusive plan C (the home where I would be molested), and plan D would be going into the foster system.

I guess it's always good to know your options…

October 19th 1993,
My Dearest Suzanne,

May the love and light you give so brilliantly to the world return to you today. So 'oft we seek to find the appropriate card, and we are blessed when those cards find us!

Divine Providence & Deep Love,
Uncle Tommy

Chapter Eighteen

Ballet Days

During the peak years of my child abuse, Mother decided it was time for a long overdue image checkup and signed me up for ballet. Much to Mother's chagrin, it did not take long for her to see I was one of the most gifted ballerinas in that studio.

"Nobody in our family has shown signs of dance talent! Where did this come from?!"

Yet, it seemed Mother had made her bed and now had to lie in it, as it were. She struggled with watching me excel in this area of the arts.

It didn't take long for her to begin fighting back. She started small. She told Father and Brother I had a mother-daughter recital so they would not come, and then she would purposely not show up either. Okay. That hurt, but it didn't stop me from bringing down the house. She could tell that I didn't get nervous on stage, which ruffled her to her core. Mother commented, *"Sweetie, I didn't get you flowers. They were so expensive."* I would just respond, *"Uh, yeah, I noticed."* I still rocked the house—flowers or no flowers.

After she saw my immense progress the next month during parents' week at the studio, things escalated even more.

Her next ballet attack came the following week when she picked me up from regular practice. From the moment I got into the car, I fastened my mental seatbelt, as I knew it would be a wild ride.

I could tell whenever Mother was trying to start a fight with me because she would always bring up my best friend, Darcy.

Not only is my daughter talented in many ways, but she knows how to keep me from her friends—an absolute outrage.

So, Mother began her random interrogations. "Suzanne, do you think I'm stupid enough to let you keep running up our telephone bill and blocking the line when I know what you're saying about me on the phone to Street-Hook Darcy? What kinds of morons do you think your father and I are? You guys have fun talking about your whore-monger adventures?"

"Hey, Mom? Sorry, I was completely blocking you out. I'm here now. It sounds like you were in the middle of one of your manipulative tactics to start a fight with me about Darcy. Did I get that right?"

In an instant, Mother turned the wheel and veered off to the side of the road before slamming on her brakes. Her fat foot hit the brake so hard that not only did I lunge forward, but about half the items in my dance bag fell to the floor. I wasn't dumb enough to bend down and pick them up off the floorboard and give her easy access to my neck. I just sat there.

*"Get out of the f***ing car."*

As I got out, I yelled, "Nobody knows why Dad won't have you committed!" Before she spun off in her station wagon, I hurled my dance bag at the side of her car and it left a dent.

Within moments, she was gone. Just like that, I was left on the side of the road.

I looked down at the scuff marks on my ballet slippers as I placed one foot in front of the other, feeling more and more desensitized with each step I took.

I certainly would have changed into walking shoes and street clothes had I known she was going to abandon me on the side of the road, leaving me both to my own devices and at the mercy of anybody who liked the idea of a young girl walking by herself on the side of the road.

Yet, there I was on one of Marietta, Georgia's busiest streets wearing a leotard and ballet tights with my dance bag slung around my shoulder. Thanks to Mother, I walked over five miles in my ballet slippers, leotard, and tights to get home. I even passed through a cemetery on the way there.

This was just another day in my life as Mother's daughter. It was not a life for the faint of heart. It was a constant war zone, and at twelve years old, I was living on the frontlines.

Mother could not lie to Father about my next performance. He already knew it was the end-of-the-year recitals, which were for entire families. She often apologized to Brother for making him go to my dance recitals. *After all, it was only me, and they were making him attend! It's not like it was his Boy Scout events or National Honor Society inductions where I was thrilled to be involved. Yeah, well, those were important because it was Brother. This was just me, and they were still making him attend—how utterly inconvenient for him.*

About a week before the year-end recitals, it was time to pick up the pictures each family had purchased for their children. To my surprise, Mother had selected a decent number of pictures. That wasn't like

Mother—she reserved the right to remain as stingy as possible on all occasions. It was their stinginess that made them so rich.

Nevertheless, Mother wanted me to come with her to pick up the pictures. I was still suspicious, but figured I had no choice but to go. On the drive there, she began picking a fight with me once again about my best friend, Darcy. Mother knew I was a loyal friend and hated it when she spoke badly of Darcy. All Mother had to do was accuse me of saying something on the phone to that "street-hook" Darcy, and it would be enough to make me mad. After all, if I was the one who was mad, anything Mother said was a justifiable result of my anger. I remember the fight lasting from the beginning of the car ride all the way to when we arrived at the photography studio.

We each got out of the car without speaking a word to one another. Although we were quiet, the intensity within each of us was boiling. Once we were inside the studio, Mother saw there were far too many parents inside for her to execute her revenge, so she quickly barked, "Sit down."

I knew she was up to something—she had not had her last word in yet—so I waited in agony for the parents to leave. We sat in those chairs for over twenty minutes, and when a representative approached us to ask if we were being helped, Mother told them, "We're waiting for someone."

That "someone" was merely a room with no parents, and she finally got her moment about five minutes later. Out of nowhere, she shot up and grabbed my arm. When we got to the table, I saw my beautiful dance pictures all laid out. Everybody else had already picked theirs up except one other girl, but Mother was willing to risk the other family seeing her. After all, it would be worth it.

"May I please have a moment alone with my daughter?" Mother oddly asked while standing at the table.

"Certainly. I'll be in the back room, and you can ring this bell when you are ready to checkout."

As the sales rep disappeared into the back room, Mother turned and glared at me. She then moved so close to me that I could see each of her mustache hairs and smell the bitter aroma of microwaved coffee on her breath. With Satan in her eyes, she hissed, *"I want you to know… You had the fattest thighs of anyone on that stage."*

"Yeah, right, you wish you could dance half as good as I can!"

With demonic fury, Mother made her move. She calmly stacked up the pictures from the largest 8 x 10s to the smallest wallet sizes and began ripping up the stack of images with deliberate mechanical movements.

I knew it was over. Tears welled up in my eyes. Mother had ripped each of my dance pictures to shreds in seconds. She picked up her oversized alligator bag and snarled, *"See you in the car."*

Father heard what happened, and a couple of days later, he had me dress back up in my recital costume so we could take some pictures of me in our hallway with the blue wallpaper background. If you look closely enough at the picture, you can see the light switch on the wall. Though Father's idea was sweet, it didn't undo the damage that Mother had done.

To this day, whenever I see a framed dance picture of a child in somebody's home, all I see is a long, white table and ripped-up pieces of ballerina me.

*"We are hard pressed on every side, but not crushed; perplexed, but not in despair; persecuted, but **not** abandoned; struck down, but not destroyed."*
-2 Corinthians 4:14 [NIV]

November 17th, 1993,
To My Sweet Suzanne,

It has become such a true honor to watch you blossom from a shy little girl in a tutu to an elegant swan on stage. You make everything up there look easy, but girl—I know it's not, because I went home and tried out some of your moves and all I know is that now I have no feeling in my left foot. Your fault. :)

All joking aside, you were the most beautiful ballerina on that stage, and it brings tears to my eyes to know that the most beautiful ballerina on that stage was the one who I came to see.

With Deep Love,
Uncle Tommy

Chapter Nineteen
"Shop Till You Drop"

*"Can a mother forget the baby at her breast and have no compassion on the child she has borne? **Though she may forget**, I will not forget you!"*
-Isaiah 49:15 [NIV]

While Mother had abused me in almost every possible way throughout my lifetime, for some reason, abandonment was always her favorite method. Whenever a new type of abuse was introduced into my life (for instance, abandonment on the side of the road), it became more frequently used in the midst of Mother's attacks. I will never forget the time Mother abandoned me on the side of the road that day after ballet class because it was the first time it happened.

There's something about "firsts" that seems to stick in the mind.

"Get out!" was always the last thing I heard before finding myself alone on the side of the road in future roadside abandonments. On the occasions when I was more than five miles from home, Mother always had enough

sense to track me down and pick me back up after she had enough time to "cool her jets". After all, she couldn't have the police getting involved. It was one thing to have suspicious neighbors, but another matter entirely to be questioned by the police. People who were questioned by the police were criminals and lowlives; Mother was above those types of people.

It didn't take long for Mother to explore all of the fun, new ways to exercise this abandonment hobby she discovered. Shopping malls seemed to be her favorite place to play.

You've heard of the concept that if you tell a lie for long enough, you start to believe it is true. This was the case when it came to Father's perception of our "shopping trips." Deep down, Father knew I would constantly be abused somehow during each of my shopping endeavors with Mother. Still, I think it made him feel better to convince himself that these trips were innocuous and legitimate mother-daughter bonding times. After all, lying to himself about the situation was much easier than facing the truth.

*"Okay, well, you girls, go have fun and **shop till you drop.**"*

How I despised hearing Father say that.

Why couldn't Father save me?! Wake up! Do something! He might as well have sent me off with a *"Bye, Suzanne! Have fun shopping with your mother until she abandons you somewhere between JCPenney and Hell!"*

Now that Mother had discovered how much fun child abandonment could be, there was not one shopping trip where I was not left alone in a crowded food court or among aisles of clothing in an unfamiliar department store. As Mother abandoned me for hours at a time on each shopping trip, I eventually got used to it and started abandoning *her.*

I beat her to the punch, in a sense, and I went ahead and abandoned myself whenever she would start to pick a fight with me. I knew she would eventually leave me, so what was the point? I saved her the trouble and started walking off on my own. I embraced the things that most children would fear with casual fearlessness. I didn't care anymore. If somebody wanted to take me, *they could have me!* The odds were, at that point, that living with a kidnapper would most likely be an improvement to my current home situation.

October 12th, 1994,
To My Sweet Spirited, Spunky, Spritely Suzanne,

I haven't heard from my favorite ballerina in a while, and I can always tell when it's time to check in with you. I am planning a Mardi Gras party for next year. Your presence is mandatory, your father's attendance would be nice, your brother's invitation was lost in the mail, and Darlene can simply stay home. Whaaaat? Who said that?

In all seriousness (as serious as it's possible for me to ever be), I would love to have you. Have your father drive you over and we'll eat junk food and stay up past curfew.

I Love You My Blue-Eyed Wonder,
Uncle Tommy

P.S. - Everything will be O.K. in the end, and even if it's not okay, it's not the end, my love.

Chapter Twenty

The Eleventh Hour

By the time I started my junior year, I was seventeen years old and my future looked pretty grim.

Isn't it like the Lord to sweep down and rescue us in the eleventh hour? The Lord is never late. He is always right on time. Of course, it is no surprise that the Lord used my beloved Godfather as a vehicle to rescue me from Mother's abuse.

Although my intrinsic fear of Mother still trumped the courage it took for me to tell my Godfather the truth, he deeply knew that things were wrong and getting worse by the day. I know now that was the Holy Spirit speaking to Tommy. He and I were so close—such kindred, united spirits—that he sensed he could not even bring the matter up because I was far too scared to talk.

Miriam had gone to be with the Lord over six years ago, so it was in these years that Tommy transformed from my kindred spirit companion to my lifelong protector, determined to keep his vow to protect me from Mother.

I'll never forget the night Tommy called my father. I was no more than a little over one month into my junior year and I had already started to live out my self-fulfilling prophecy of being a C student at best. I had never wanted to pick up one of the phones in the house and listen in as badly as I did then. However, I knew Tommy was on the line, and I refused to ever do anything to compromise his trust.

As I waited, I embarked upon a noble endeavor to fit more than a single eight and a half by eleven-inch sheet of paper onto the dilapidated, paint-chipped teal desk Mother bought me for schoolwork. I always pictured it being featured on one of those National Geographic documentaries where they uncovered carnage from the maiden voyage of the RMS Titanic.

Most of the time, I chipped off the paint until I either fell asleep or had to pee.

I was set up for success!

About an hour after chipping a successful pile of paint onto the floor, I heard Father walking up the stairs. I quickly grabbed my geography book and opened it on the surface of my shipwrecked furniture. *Let's see, page forty-seven seems like a relevant chapter to be in. Hopefully, he won't ask what I'm working on, because I would have the same question for him.*

Father opened my bedroom door in a way where I could tell we were about to have a serious talk.

"Hey, Sweetie, wanna take a break and sit with me on the bed for a minute?"

I figured I could rest from my busy hours of scrupulously chipping paint off my Titanic desk.

When I joined Father on the bed, for just a small moment, it felt like I was a little girl again. I missed those days when he picked me up out of bed, carried me down the stairs, and put me into the car before sunrise as we left for our summer vacations.

Sometimes, it's the most unadorned memories that we often hold most dear.

"I was just on the phone with your Uncle Tommy, and he told me about a school his friend's daughter attends."

The conversation abruptly shifted.

School? A new school? Were we moving?

"It's a boarding school in North Georgia, and it seems highly accredited in both academics and athletics."

Oh, a boarding school. We weren't moving; they were shipping me off. At first, I scoffed at the idea of me being some problem child to send off.

I wasn't the problem, it was Mother! Send *her* to some reform school!

After the dust had settled and a few days had passed, I approached Father one evening before bed.

I'm sure this was the last thing he expected to come out of my mouth, but as I stood in the doorway, I looked him straight in the eye and said:

"I'll go."

He closed his book and looked at me with conflicting expressions of both confusion and deep joy.

"You know, once I sign you up, there's no turning back, and you are enrolled to live there. Have you thought this through?"

For the first time in my life, it felt like Father was speaking to me like somebody he respected. It's like I was Daddy's girl again but matured. I felt like he saw me for the first time in years outside of the brainwashing he received from the daily hate Mother spewed.

By this time, I had already made my share of mistakes. I saw this as an opportunity not only for a fresh start, but to be free from Mother's abuse.

It was my ticket out. I took it.

Within only two weeks, Father and I had taken a full tour of the campus and my application had officially been accepted. My last day at public school was approaching, and by the first week of November, I was fully moved in as a full-time boarding school student on campus.

It wasn't until later that I realized this was Father's first major decision without Mother. Boy, did she resent him for this one! I'm not sure if she has ever forgiven Father to this day, for he found a way to set Mother's prisoner free.

Chapter Twenty-One
Boarding School & The Two-Year Escape

"For He will conceal me when troubles come; He will hide me in his sanctuary. He will place me out of reach on a high rock."
-Psalm 27:5 [NLT]

While I could not wait to finally live free from Mother's violent regime, I was not at all prepared for what God was about to show me next.

For the next two years, I went from living a self-fulfilling prophecy as a C student to making the Dean's list and being inducted into the National Honor Society. Despite the verbal poison Mother spewed at me each day, once I got away from her, I realized that I'm actually not stupid and I'm certainly not worthless. I realized that I am bright and have a fantastic future ahead of me. I was told lies, and even though they weren't true, I lived them out because that's what I believed about myself.

Even though God had this perfect purpose for me since birth, He went above and beyond to show me just how valuable I am. I maintained an over 100% average in chemistry, organic chemistry, English, and calculus.

I went from being the one who needed a tutor to being the tutor. I was so confident, intelligent, and so funny that I even took my AP English college exam while wearing a wig just because someone dared me to. My teachers were used to my shenanigans. That wig did not distract me, and I tested out of all my freshman English courses. I was encouraged. People saw me—the real me.

Once I was away from Mother's grip, I realized I was hilarious. Technically, I *knew* I was hilarious, but God finally gave me the context to let it shine. I received (with utmost pride) the "Class Clown" senior superlative, and I loved it. I loved it because it was true but I still made all A's. I remember Mother being so disappointed that I got "Class Clown." She wanted me to get "Most Likely to Succeed." I didn't need a superlative to

tell me I would succeed. My, how Mother truly missed the boat with me.

Not only was I hilarious, but I was compassionate and intelligent. This powerful combination allowed me to eat lunch at any table—from the most popular kids to the foreign exchange students. It's like I could make anyone my people. My boarding school roommate and I were best friends. She was like Wednesday Addams. Bright, yet her favorite color was black, and she didn't talk to people.

But then she met me.

I got her to open up.

God opened up a whole new path in my heart. I connected with her on an intellectual level first, only to later realize that she was hilarious, too. Not everyone could see it, but I saw it, and I made a point to let her know that I loved the Wednesday Addams side of her, but that she was also so much more.

God further showed me how valuable I am by allowing me to shine in track and cross-country. I broke school records for the triple jump, the 400 meter, the 300 meter hurdles (I continuously broke my own record in this event at every meet my senior year), and I was the girls' MVP for cross-country my junior and senior year.

In public school, I didn't even make the track team.

God was proving a point. He showed me that I was none of the things Mother told me I was.

"For we are his workmanship, created in Christ Jesus for good works, which God prepared beforehand, that we should walk in them."
-Ephesians 2:10 [ESV]

Chapter Twenty-Two

High School Graduation

"'For I know the plans I have for you,' declares the LORD, 'Plans to prosper you and not to harm you, plans to give you hope and a future."
-Jeremiah 29:11 [NIV]

Before I knew it, high school graduation was upon me. In just two short years, I went from having an uncertain future to graduating high school with multiple college acceptance letters. I accepted an offer to a private liberal arts school in South Carolina. I joined the university with a part-academic part-athletic scholarship, and I had already tested out of all my freshman English courses. I was already set up in the work/study program to serve as an English tutor at the university.

The above picture is probably my favorite photo of Tommy and me. A snapshot in time. A single moment in eternity. I was, in every way possible, on top of the world as I stood smiling with my biggest supporter while wearing my cap and gown—an outfit I never imagined donning.

I suppose this is one of those times I can look back and see that all the signs from God were there, but I did my own thing. I seemed to overlook that I had inherited the gift of writing from Father's side of the family.

You see, I always knew I was gifted in writing and English classes, I just didn't have the encouragement

living under Mother's rule to apply myself. Therefore, for me, it was nothing short of amazing that I maintained A+ averages in any math or science courses.

Don't get me wrong; there is nothing wrong with acknowledging my outstanding work in the sciences and committing myself to becoming a pre-med student intent on studying neuroscience. It was a noble endeavor. The only problem was that I had not checked in with the man upstairs.

In those days, I believed in God but still was not remotely close to understanding Scripture and the nature of God himself as I would in my adult years. I prayed at night and kept the belief in my heart that he was real. Yet, as I was not brought up in the Word, that was probably about as best as I could do.

Looking back, I now see that all the signs were there for me to pursue a career in writing; I just could not see them. Some of the best lessons we learn are from the experience of mistakes made.

Despite multiple acceptance letters from prestigious universities, I declined my number one choice and chose to attend the same college as Brother.

Finally, he would see me. Finally, he would love me. Finally, he would want to spend time with me. Finally, he would look at me the same way he looked at his friends. Finally.

A couple of months after choosing to attend Brother's school, I received the most heart-shattering news of my life. Despite my amazing, jaw-dropping accomplishment, Mother and Father did not find it necessary that Brother even attend my high school graduation. To this day, I cannot figure out which was more heartbreaking: the fact that Mother and Father did not make him go, or the fact that he did not even *want* to go.

I went to his lackluster, unsurprising graduation—celebrating his lofty achievements made from work done on his executive-style mahogany wood schoolwork desk. Mother and Father did not make Brother attend my graduation, however, because he was away working in Yellowstone for the summer and would have to pay for a plane ticket to fly home.

Apparently, Mother and Father couldn't seem to swing the cost of a round-trip plane ticket home to celebrate my graduation, yet, they paid for my private boarding school. Sounds legit.

May 27th, 1999,
My Dearest Suzanne,

You did it, baby!!! Congratulations to my high school graduate and college-bound baby Suzanne! I remain astounded at your academic and athletic prowess. I think back to all of the troubled times you had in that house and when things were anything but well—then came your new school! Your boarding school was the perfect atmosphere you needed to get away from all of the things pulling you down and see your true potential. You, my love, did exactly that. You have climbed to academic and athletic achievements that were so far beyond what was anticipated. I marvel at your accomplishments, and I could not be a prouder Godfather!

Words continue to fail to properly express how utterly proud I am for you—though I have been proud of you since your birth. As you continue to steamroll through chemistry, calculus, and such, don't forget to stoke those creative juices! You have the most wonderful creative imaginative mind. Please continue to author those creative stories in joy and romance.

I Love You Dearly,
Uncle Tommy

"ME"

The highway to intelligence is wise,
Crowded and Clamorous;
Fraught with ambition
And marked by trial and error.

The path to wisdom is narrow, lonely, and quiet;
Littered with pain,
Bordered and embroidered by acquiescence.

I know many things.
But, as yet,
I do not know enough
To know that
Which I do not know!

And, therein lies the rub.

In all thy getting,
Get understanding.

-Benjamin F. Doster

Part Four
The Young Adult Years

Chapter Twenty-Three
Checking Out

It was September 11th, 2001, and my dreams began shattering alongside the fabric of our entire nation. God rest the souls of the helpless Americans trapped inside those blazing buildings. As I watched in horror on my dorm room television screen, I was also desperate to escape and couldn't find a way out.

Anybody who is old enough to remember the September 11, 2001, terrorist attacks on the Twin Towers remembers what they were doing the exact moment they heard the news.

It was a Tuesday morning; I was a junior in college preparing to attend medical school for neuroscience with a 4.0 GPA. Things seemed to be going perfectly for me both academically and socially, as I was an upperclassman member of one of the campus's Christian sororities. Indeed, things were going quite well for me in the life plan that I chose for myself.

In those days, I had adopted the "work hard, play hard" mentality, and that Tuesday morning was when the partying started to catch up with me. The weekend before, I had been driven to the hospital by some sorority sisters to treat a suspected case of alcohol poisoning. While they did not need to pump my stomach, it is safe to say that it was reckless for me to allow myself to succumb to such a condition.

Growing up, I had never really been taught too much about the physical and spiritual dangers of intoxication. All I knew was that Mother had grown up Southern Baptist and refused to even have a glass of wine on special occasions due to her religion. At age twenty, I thought that was dumb, and college allowed me to show myself just how foolish Mother was. One of the "Godisms" I often spoke was, "You can't judge what's in my heart by what's in my cup." In case you were wondering, a "Godism" is something people say that is found nowhere in Scripture. Looking back, I can see Jesus popping his head out from the corner, saying, "I never said that."

On the morning of the September 11, 2001 attacks, I woke up to a phone call from the Dean of students notifying me that he needed to meet with me in his office. While the Dean did not specify the nature of the meeting, I was pretty sure it involved the events from the prior weekend.

I threw some jeans and a sweatshirt on, quickly brushed my teeth, grabbed the keys to my 1998 black Toyota Camry, and headed to the academic hall where I was to meet the Dean. The moment I walked into the meeting, not only did I feel underdressed, but I was underprepared. The Dean of students failed to mention that the entire social board of my campus sorority and my best friend, Rachel, would be present.

Rachel? Why was Rachel there? I tried to make eye contact with her, but it proved impossible as her eyes were glued to the floor. Rachel was one of my sorority sisters who had cared for me and drove me to the hospital. What was she doing here? Why wasn't she looking up?

The meeting was short, dry, and cut right to the chase. I learned that I would be placed on social probation in my sorority as a result of my irresponsible behavior. If I wanted to remain an active sister in my sorority, I was banned from visiting any fraternity house on campus. I was not to consume a drop of alcohol, nor was I to be seen even holding an alcoholic beverage or attend any social events hosted by my sorority until further notice. I signed some forms acknowledging that I understood the terms of my probation and left the meeting. As I exited the building, I waited for my best friend Rachel. Any moment now, she would come right out of those main doors and start laughing about what a colossal joke this all was.

Five minutes passed. No Rachel.

Ten minutes passed. No Rachel.

I was starting to get cold, and I had to pee. What was taking her so long?

Then, I got the worst feeling in the pit of my stomach.

It was at that moment that I realized Rachel wasn't coming. She wouldn't be walking out with me. Something was wrong; she was my best friend and would never dare betray me like this… right?

Though I knew something was off, I could not afford to wait outside any longer if I wanted to make it in time to my 10:00 A.M. cell biology class. I hadn't missed a class yet and wouldn't start now.

I turned the keys in the ignition and drove back to my dorm. It was on the drive home that I heard the reports of the first plane hitting the World Trade Center's North building.

That's horrible. A plane actually hit the World Trade Center? What in the world could have gone wrong? What a crazy accident!

Yet, I couldn't figure out why this story was on every radio station. It seemed like the news had taken over the radio that morning.

I slowly transitioned back into my bubble of problems that morning— social probation. Okay, it couldn't be that bad, right? All of this was dumb. Surely, my sorority sister suitemates and Rachel would help me navigate this mess. They must have brainwashed her in that meeting, but everything will be fine and we'll go back to normal as soon as I can get her alone.

When I parked at my dormitory and shut off the car, I realized I had left my student ID in my dorm room and was locked out. Standing at the double doors to my dorm, I pressed the call button to my room. One of my suitemates, Sarah, answered. "Hello?"

"Hey Sarah, it's Suzanne. I forgot my ID card. Could you buzz me in?" I heard some commotion in the background and asked, "What's going on?"

"The South World Trade Center just collapsed, and the first one is not looking good."

"Wait… what do you mean the second building? I thought there was just one accident?"

"You need to keep your ID card on you more," Sarah barked, and I was buzzed in.

As I opened the door to my room, I could hear the television from outside the door. I was ready to find out what exactly was happening in New York. Sarah looked at me plainly and said, "This looks like World War III." To this day, I'm still uncertain if she was commenting on the state of our nation, our friendship, or perhaps a little bit of both.

I looked down at my desk and saw a written notice signed by my other three sorority sister suitemates informing me that I had until the end of the month to find a new place to live.

Just then, I looked up from the paper, and the North tower officially collapsed.

As it turned out, I never had a chance to speak to Rachel face to face, and I had become a social pariah in both the sorority and fraternity circles. I was forced to move into a random freshman dormitory as a junior: complete social suicide.

It did not take long for the combination of all the social pressure to begin affecting my academics. I went from a 4.0 student to someone who stopped going to class. I stopped doing anything. I stopped sleeping, I stopped leaving my dorm room, I even stopped eating. My grades were so high in each class before the social and academic crises that I stayed in bed the rest of that semester and still came home that Christmas with all C's.

I remember being at the kitchen table over Christmas break, begging Mother and Father to transfer me to another school. I just needed a fresh start—a change of scenery. Mother and Father both knew how hard of a worker I was, so it made them scratch their heads a bit. Ultimately, it came down to the most profound emotional appeal a daughter could make to her parents. I was on my knees, begging not to return to that school.

Much to my surprise, Father lifted his finger and decreed that I return to the university. Since when did Father make any types of decisions?

I knew this would be a disaster, but there was nothing I could say to either Mother or Father to get them to side with me.

Christmas came and went, and I helplessly returned to the university like a wounded, lost sheep with nowhere to go. Classes started, and the same thing began happening—or *not* happening, I should say. I could not get out of bed. I wanted to be asleep all day. When I was awake, I lay in bed wishing I were asleep. This time, I did not have a two-month buffer of all A's to coast off of. I was making zeroes in all of my classes.

By February, my parents received a phone call from the university Dean asking my father to pick me up. I had been taken by the school psychologist to a local psychiatric facility and had been diagnosed and treated for severe depression and anorexia.

I rested in the passenger seat as Father drove me away. As the campus university became smaller and smaller in the rearview mirror, so did my dreams of one day becoming a neuroscientist. Perhaps all was not lost, however. I finally got Mother and Father to side with me. I finally got Father to let me leave the university. As I turned to Father, for the first time in my life, I saw tears welling up in his eyes. At that moment, everything was such a blur to me. I didn't know what to think of anything for the time being. The only thought I remember coming to my mind after seeing Father's tears was, *Perhaps this means I'm his little girl again.*

Many sorority sisters stood by my side during this time and for years to come. As to Rachael and my suitemates, they were never heard from again.

February 23rd, 2002,
My Dearest Suzanne,

I think about you daily. Your father tells me that things didn't go quite as you had planned at the university. I know it may be hard to hear right now, but in my spirit, I sense that God has a different plan for my sweet Suzanne. Please don't worry about all of that right now though, and just focus on getting our sweet Suzanne better. I've got your best interests at heart, so don't worry about anything. I've got your back. It took your Uncle Tommy the better part of a decade to graduate from college.

I'll call you next week when you have had a little more time to rest, baby girl.

With Deep Love,
Uncle Tommy

Want to Hear A Good Definition of Success?

"To laugh often and love much; to win the respect of intelligent persons and the affection of children; to earn to approbation of honest citizens and endure the betrayal of false friends; to appreciate beauty; to find the best in others; to give of one's self;

To leave the world a bit better, whether by a healthy child, a garden patch, or a redeemed social condition; to have played and laughed with enthusiasm and sung with exultation; to know that even one life has breathed easier because you have lived: this is to have succeeded."

-Ralph Waldo Emerson

The Great Falling Away

To this day, it remains one of my life's biggest ironies that I lost all of my faith at a Christian college. In my mind, attending the same college as Brother would bring us closer. In my mind, attending a Christian college would bring me closer to God.

I suppose this happens when you plan your life without bothering to consult God.

Looking back, I resign my crisis of faith to two areas: my inability to separate people from Christianity and a misguided discipleship.

Perhaps one of the greatest tragedies of humanity is our tendency to associate "Christians" with "Christianity." I know from personal experience how easy of a trap this can be, especially when you have made only one social group of Christians your entire world. I have learned to be kinder to younger me, for I understand where I came from. With no firm foundation or exposure to solid Christians growing up, I had no choice but to place all of my eggs in one basket with my Christian sorority. Without a solid background in true Christianity, I could only reflect on my experience with my Christian sorority. I said to myself, "If this is Christianity, I want absolutely nothing to do with it."

And so, for a very long time, I didn't.

That's the thing about being hurt by other Christians. No matter how hurt you have become in the context of the church or Christianity, it doesn't make God's love for us or the gospel of Jesus Christ any less true. This is a profound truth that took me almost a decade to embrace.

These days, when I am discipling those newer in Christianity or those who do not believe, I like to discern truth from the *essence* of truth. For instance, the truth could be that you are reading this book. It's a statement that reflects a fact. Chances are, if you have gotten this far, you are likely to continue reading and even finish this book. There are, however, no spiritual laws set in place that guarantee this truth. At any moment, you could receive a phone call or text that might claim your attention for a moment and change this truth—even for just a moment.

There is only one *essence* of truth, and that is found in The Holy Bible: the gospel of Jesus Christ. The words in this book are elevated to a separate dimension of truth because there is nothing in the natural world that can ever change the truth behind these words.

The matter of discipleship was the second factor that contributed to my personal decision to question Christianity as a whole in my early twenties. I praise the Lord that the issue of proper discipleship is something I can become better and not bitter about. It is my experience with my Christian sorority that eventually caused me to become passionate about correct, careful discipleship.

The issue for me in those days revolved around my perception of being judged as a bad Christian because I had no problem drinking and getting intoxicated after a hard week of schoolwork.

The truth is, I wasn't modeling the behavior of a good Christian. The Bible tells us to not get drunk with wine, but to be filled instead with the Holy Spirit. So, my sorority sisters were right. The problem was that they weren't discipling with humility or love, and it resulted in me turning from Christianity altogether. As I look back on those sorority sisters' harsh attempts to disciple me, I am fully convinced that they meant well and did not intend for me to turn from Christianity. They were still young in their faith, too. Nobody had taught them that there was a better way to disciple—Jesus's way of discipling.

Scripture is filled with examples of how we should properly disciple one another. Notice the regenerative effect of discipleship. We are not called to make converts. We are called to make disciples so those we teach can go and teach others.

Jesus Christ was very intentional in how he discipled in the days of his ministry on Earth. He discipled with *humility* and *love.* He dined with the sinners and tax collectors. He did not elevate himself over anyone, even though he could have. He was intentional to meet people where they were in life. His method was, quite frankly, brilliant. By leveling himself with the lowly and socially downtrodden, He gained their trust. When others began to trust Him, they could see and feel Jesus's love. We know from the Bible that love conquers all. Once those under his teachings felt his passion, it was only a matter of time before their hearts changed as well. Jesus, the son of God, never forced anyone to accept him (and never will). This is where free will comes in. Even with the proper discipleship model from Jesus, it was always up to the other person to decide to become transformed by the love of Jesus Christ.

Along with being my lifetime protector and encourager, Tommy was one of the most "Jesus-y" people I had ever met. He took the Great Commission seriously. Like Jesus, Tommy spent a lifetime humbling himself and showing love to the lost by placing them in a position to receive the good news of the gospel of Jesus Christ. Like Jesus, Tommy discipled from a place of love and humility—not fear or judgment.

One of my favorite pictures of Tommy is him sitting down and breaking bread with Muslims on an overseas mission trip. I look at that picture and smile. I know I wasn't there for the conversation, but it makes me proud to know he was breaking bread with them to show them love and place himself in a proper position to share about Jesus. He wasn't always accepted, but as a true disciple of Jesus Christ, he never passed up a chance to share about Jesus.

My Godfather Tommy breaking bread with a group of Muslims on an overseas mission trip.

Disciple Through Love and Humility

"While Jesus was having dinner at Matthew's house, many tax collectors and sinners came and ate with him and his disciples. When the Pharisees saw this, they asked his disciples, 'Why does your teacher eat with tax collectors and sinners'? On hearing this, Jesus said, 'It is not the healthy who need a doctor, but the sick... For I have not come to call the righteous, but sinners."
-Matthew 9:10-17 [NIV]

"Therefore, let us stop passing judgment on one another. Instead, make up your mind not to put any stumbling block or obstacle in the way of a brother or sister."
-Romans 14:13 [NIV]

"If I speak in the tongues of men or angels, but do not have love, I am only a resounding gong of a clanging cymbal."
-I Corinthians 1:3 [NIV]

"A new commandment I give you: Love one another. As I have loved you, so you must love one another. By this, everyone will know that you are my disciples, if you love one another."
-James 13:34 & 35 [NIV]

"And now these three remain: faith, hope and love. But the greatest of these is love."
-1 Corinthians 13:13 [NIV]

July 16th 2003,
To My Beloved Suzanne,

I pray for you daily, my sweet love, Please know that I understand where things are for you right now in the spiritual department. I don't want you to think that I am judging you or looking down on you in any respect. Please erase that thought from your mind. Simply put, don't go there! I know what things are like for you as someone with natural creative talent who, quite possibly, feels as though she is being imprisoned within the very walls in which she must reside. I know it must not be easy for you being back in the home with your Mother when you want to spread your wings and fly.

As to the spiritual bit, there is only one question I have for you at this time. As someone who has loved you from your birth, I feel as though I have at least earned the right to ask you this singular question at this "paused" chapter of your life:

Is your life better or worse without God?

With Deep Love,
Uncle Tommy

P.S. - God has always been as good to me as I would let him be.

Chapter Twenty-Five
Trust

Living back at home with Mother in my early twenties was soul-shattering. Every day, I would think back on my surprising peak during those two glorious years at boarding school where God showed me my true potential.

Here I was—a college dropout, no longer pre-med, and living back home with Mother and Father. You can imagine the complete nosedive my self-esteem took.

Mother pitied me when I first returned home and decided to wait almost an entire month before abusing me again. Somewhere in between the derogatory names and the punches thrown, perhaps the biggest tragedy thus far occurred: I slowly reverted to the old, abused image of myself. No matter how hard I forced my brain to try and remember who God showed me to be at boarding school, I could not access this former view of myself and continued, once again, to live out the self-fulfilling prophecies spoken over me by Mother.

I wasn't sure what I would do, nor how (if ever) I could truly understand who God showed me I was. As an adult, I was now too old to be rescued by any school or government agency.

I was on my own.

Life without God is dark. It is devoid of any semblance of hope or truth. That is the place in which I now lived.

So there I was—age twenty-four with seventy-five percent of my college degree complete but no plans to finish and return. It was bad enough to be living at home with Mother and Father at this age and working as a waitress at Joe's Crab Shack. Even worse, I was back in the horrific vortex of abuse. Perhaps I felt less sorry for myself because I was no longer a child. After all, nobody talks about "adult child abuse," right? Maybe I was old enough to suck it up.

Perhaps the only perk of returning home was being closer to Tommy and seeing him more often. He spent much time with me during those days, trying his best to spiritually and emotionally redirect me amid my quarter-life crisis.

At least once a month, Tommy would take me out to dinner and we would have some of our best talks.

One particular dinner has always stood out in my mind, and I'm sure it also stayed in Tommy's. Tommy always let me pick the restaurant, and this time, I had chosen Sidelines Bar and Grill in downtown Marietta, Georgia. I remember the conversation started just after the waitress had taken our orders and walked back to the kitchen.

Tommy was discussing how Father and I felt like my boarding school years were the years in which I truly shined the brightest, and he told me how much he knew I would return to that place in my life. At the time, I struggled to believe him, but I still held on to a glimmer of hope that his words would come to pass deep down in my innermost spirit.

A few moments had passed by as we waited for our food when Tommy transitioned into talking about Father in his early years before I was born.

Tommy and Father initially met at college; they were fraternity brothers and best friends. It is interesting to look back on Tommy's relationship with Father and see the shift as Mother slowly took the wheel. Neither Tommy nor Mimi had ever been a fan of Mother's. Even back in the days when Mother still had friends, they saw straight through her. They both naturally had a highly intuitive nature, which I am thankful for because it led to a lifetime of them protecting me as best as they could from Mother.

I was now an adult, and Tommy (a healthy, non-abusive role model) started treating me like a parent should treat an adult child. Our relationship slowly transitioned from parent and child to parent and friend. Tommy began to open up to me as a friend might, and he started trusting me with confidential facts as I slowly opened up to him.

Tommy was becoming my friend!

That particular night, Tommy chose to reminisce about the early days of his friendship with Father. How I loved hearing these tales. It's almost as if I never truly knew my father. By the time I was born, his true identity was already being swallowed by Mother's. By the time I was twenty-four, Father had become an extension of her. Indeed, it is a Biblical truth that two become one in the union of marriage. Unfortunately, in the case of Father, this union went in the wrong direction—as they both became Mother.

Tommy began telling a funny tale about one night when Father had made a mistake and had too much to drink. "Let me tell you, Suzanne, your Father was *comatose* in the backseat of my Ford pickup! It's funny when I think about it now, for I haven't seen that side of your Father since his first marriage with Julia."

His words seemed to come out slower than the rest, and I stared at him blankly as if he had suddenly started speaking in Chinese.

"Hello, Earth-to-Suzanne? What's with the face, doll?"

I just continued to stare at him; I even stopped chewing the bread that was in my mouth. To this day, I cannot imagine what my face looked like on the receiving end, but I'm sure it expressed deep alarm and complete confusion.

Finally, I found the strength to muster up a group of words and combine them into a comprehensive sentence.

"Who is Julia?"

The time between my question and Tommy's response seemed to last an eternity. His entire countenance immediately changed, and I could tell something was seriously wrong. The look on his face told me that he had unintentionally spoken out of turn. His eyes went from deep confusion to sympathy, and instead of talking, he decided to say to me, "Keep talking, love."

At that point, it had become apparent that Tommy had somehow inadvertently opened an entire can of worms and now we were both trying our best to sort through the mess.

"I know nobody named Julia, Tommy," I said with increasing alarm. "What are you saying? My dad was married before?"

Tommy let me continue asking the questions out loud to get everything out of my system. He didn't say much else on the topic that evening, for he knew I already had enough to process in my mind.

At age twenty-four, I found out from Father's best friend that he had been married before he met Mother.

That night, I was unable to sleep. I tossed and turned. It was not the fact that Father had a previous marriage that I was angry about. It was the fact that he and Mother kept it a secret from Brother and me.

The next day, I secretly placed a telephone call to Mother's mother. I have not spoken much of Mother's mother to this point, as all I know is that she abused Mother. She was a curious, cold woman, and I had never been close to her. She was not exactly the type of grandmother who would bake me cookies and give me hugs. I'm not sure if I've ever even touched Grandmother.

The phone began to ring. After three rings, I heard a distinct "ye-llow" with a downward inflection.

I always wanted to follow that with "Blue! Orange! Pink!" but I behaved.

I didn't sugarcoat a thing nor waste a moment. I went straight in: "Grandmother, was Mother married before she met Father?"

"What? Who, you mean Chuck?"

Silence on my end.

"Hello? Suzanne—I said hello! Why are you asking about Chuck?"

"So, she was… married before Father to a… man named Chuck?" I confirmed.

"Well, yeah," Grandmother stated plainly. After that, she said, "You didn't know that?"

I was done. I hung up the receiver and disconnected the cord from the wall so she could not call back. I didn't care if I would be beaten for disrespecting Grandmother. What's another punch in the face these days, after all? I figured I would deal with the consequences of my actions later.

I ran across the hall, shut the door to my bedroom, and placed my face into a pillow. I began to yell. Then, I screamed even louder.

After I had calmed down a little bit, the same questions began to enter my mind.

Why was such a seemingly mundane fact kept hidden all these years? Why did they not respect me enough to be forthright with me about who they were and use it as a teaching moment like any other healthy parent/ adult child relationship would? Why was I hearing of each of my parents' previous marriages from third parties and not directly from them? If they had intentionally kept their previous marriages a secret for so many years, what *else* were they hiding?

Did they each secretly commit some wretched crime in their previous marriages? Did Brother and I secretly have half-siblings we don't even know about? Who even were they anymore? How could I possibly trust them moving forward in life?

I wasted no time at all confronting them each on the issue. Father was at work and not to be bothered, but lucky me, Mother was home.

I went downstairs to the living room where Mother watched her favorite show, Judge Judy. At least some semblance of justice was being represented in that house—even if it was through a tawdry show.

"Why didn't you and Dad tell me you guys have each had previous marriages?"

Mother was silent but muted the television. Apparently, this conversation wasn't even worthy enough for her to completely turn it off. She still had to watch the show's verdict.

It was time for Mother to speak the only language she knew how to speak: abuse.

"Listen here, you little whore-monger. The last time I checked, I'm covering your room and board, and you're the little slut still living with your parents. I refuse to be bothered with harassing facts about our lives. Go make yourself useful."

Well, that went as expected.

I left the room but stayed around long enough to hear Judge Judy's verdict. "Guilty." Too bad Judge Judy didn't live here.

At that point in my life, Mother and Father had purchased a Nokia cell phone for me to use in case of emergencies coming to and from work. I wasn't working, but this was an emergency.

I opened the top drawer of my dresser, grabbed the phone, and powered it on. Ugh, my inbox was full—time to empty my texts. I waited four to five minutes to empty my text inbox, and even that seemed like an eternity to me.

Finally, "Inbox (0)" showed up on the screen.

I texted Brother the information I had learned. At this point in his life, he had already graduated from the university we both attended and Mother and Father had directed him to the insurance industry. He was working in Macon, Georgia as a commercial insurance agent. How lovely for him.

Like my call with Grandmother, I did not waste time sugarcoating anything. "Just so you know, both Mom and Dad have had previous marriages and have been lying to us our entire lives."

There was no response.

Later that night, Father came home from work and sat down at the foot of my bed as if I were an unruly teenager once again and he was about to discipline me.

"I heard what you said to your Brother, and I want you to know that really hurt him, Suzanne." Father spoke. Father left the room, and to this day, the subject matter was never spoken of again.

Honesty is Always the Best Policy…

"Lying lips are an abomination to the LORD, but those who deal truthfully are His delight."
-Proverbs 12:22 (NKJV)

"Better is the poor that wallets in his integrity than he that is perverse in his lips, and is a fool."
-Proverbs 19:1 (KJV)

"For we are taking pains to do what is right not only in the eyes of the LORD, but also in the eyes of man."
-2 Corinthians 8:21 (NIV)

"Do your best to present yourself to God as one approved, aworker who does not need to be ashamed."
-2 Timothy 2:15 (NIV)

"Do not lie to each other, since you have taken off your old self with its practices."
-Colossians 3:9 (NIV)

"Put off falsehood and speak truthfully to your neighbor, for we are all members of one body."
-Ephesians 4:25 [NIV]

October 22nd 2004,

To Suzanne, My "Diamond in the Rough,"

Hello to my sweet Suzy! I have been thinking about you much since our last dinner date. Your mother (and quite recently) your father have become studies of confusion in my eyes. The fact that they kept secret each of their previous marriages remains a complete mystery to me. I have known your mother for many August moons, and your father seems to be losing more and more of his true identity the longer they are together. I am happy they found one another, because I know this world needed you. Nevertheless, I would be remiss if I did not say there are times when I just miss my old friend. The more time that goes by, the less faith I have in getting my old comrade back.

I am honored that God has given each of us things we have longed for in our friendship. You are desiring a parent who will treat you as an adult, and I find myself longing for a daughter who will want to spend time with me, or at least just call me on my birthday.

God works out our pain for good. I believe our special friendship is a perfect example of his goodness in each of our lives.

Wherever thou goest, I am with thee... 'till your personal, wonderful conclusion,

Uncle Tommy

P.S. - It takes a long time to grow an old friend, and—in our case—it was certainly well worth the wait!

Chapter Twenty-Six

Christmas Morning Alone

In my lifetime, I could always have as much or as little of God as I wanted. 2005 marks the lowest spiritual time in my life. It's safe to say that is when I chose to have the very least amount of God. By that time, I had been working for long enough to save up for a down payment on a one-bedroom apartment, and as soon as I was able, I was out the door.

As it turns out, apartment life was not as glamorous as I made it out to be in my mind. When you don't have God, you keep looking for worldly places to fill the gap. My God-sized void was constantly being filled with one failed romantic relationship after another. If I couldn't have the deepest, primal love from the maker of the universe, then I would substitute it with a cheap romance. Sometimes, they broke my heart. Other times, I broke their hearts. Either way, one thing stayed the same—none seemed to last long.

One significant part of apartment living, however, was that I did not communicate with Mother. Deep down, I kept thinking that being away from that house would once again do what boarding school did for me.

The longer I went with less and less life success, the more confused I became. It happened before. Why wasn't it happening again? What was missing?

God was missing.

This, of course, is where free will comes in. You see, at boarding school, I was not the most devout Christian, but that was no fault of my own. I wasn't raised the right way, but I still believed in my heart. God honored that belief, and look at how amazingly he stretched my mustard seed faith! That's the funny thing about mustard seeds: though incredibly small, they have the potential to grow into giant trees.

Though I would never admit it at the time, deep down, I was expecting God to move in my apartment days. God wasn't the problem; I was the problem. You see, God cannot and will not move in our lives unless we give him room. By that point, I had blatantly rejected God, yet I was still expecting him to bless me. God was honoring my free will in dismissing him.

You can't have your cake and eat it, too.

By the time the holidays came around, I was barely functional. The Godless version of me was basically like a walking zombie just going through the motions. Godless me was also incredibly selfish. I cared about me and my needs—nobody else's.

I remember having the majority of the week of Christmas off of work. Mother, Father, Brother, and I would get together on Christmas Eve. It was the one night of the year when we were allowed to sit at the dining room table and eat. Mother would dim the lights and light candles, and a wonderful feast was always prepared with Tchaikovsky's *Nutcracker* softly playing in the background. As Brother and I grew older, Mother and Father stopped taking us to Christmas Eve service as much. They thought, *Well, they're adults now—what's the point?* Make no mistake, though, no matter how old Brother and I got, we were still lavished richly throughout the years on Christmas morning. Christmas was Mother's one opportunity to shine. She could manipulate her way into pretending there was love in that house. Christmas was always huge.

After all, there's always Christmas, right?

It was the year I spent Christmas Eve and Christmas morning alone that made me realize I had hit absolute rock bottom.

A fight had broken out over the phone between Mother and me when she reminded me to "hold in that tummick'" (her stupid way of saying stomach) so I could fit into my dress.

"I don't know what the point is; we never even end up going. We haven't attended church on Christmas Eve for five years. And maybe you should hold in that size twenty 'tummick' of yours," I rebutted.

To no surprise, I heard her hang up the phone. I didn't even bother to reach back out. This is where my gruesome selfishness came in because I turned my phone off and left it off all the way through to December 27th. It's like I shut off the entire world.

Christmas morning by myself was the saddest I have ever been in my life. After that experience, I knew it was time for a change.

Even in this moment where I felt the most alone in my life, the word of God tells me I was never alone.

"Where can I go from your Spirit? Where can I flee from your presence? If I go up to the heavens, you are there; if I make my bed in the depths, you are there. If I rise on the wings of the dawn, if I settle on the far side of the sea, even there, your hand will guide me, your right hand will hold me fast."
-Psalm 139:7-10 (NIV)

Hunting Island Flashback: Still the Same Free Spirit

December 23rd 2006,
Merry Christmas My Sweet Suzanne!

Another year finished and a new one on the horizon. Early this morning, I was driving to work, and these words just hit me: "all is calm."

What a quiet joy it was to witness an apparent pause to the much expected mayhem. Perhaps, this next year, we can each unwind and sense:

"How quietly, how quietly, the wondrous gift is given!"

Joyeux Noel, My Love,
Uncle Tommy

"When love is felt or fear is known,
When holidays and holy days
And such times come,
When anniversaries arrive
By calendar or consciousness
When seasons come, as seasons do,
Old and known, but somehow new.
When lives are born,
Or people die,
When something sacred's sensed
In soil or sky.
MARK THE TIME.
Respond with thought, or prayer
Or smile or grief.
Let nothing living
Life or leaf
Slip between the fingers of the mind.
For all of these are holy things
We will not, cannot, find again."

-Mark A. Coots

Chapter Twenty-Seven

Lost and Found

*"If you return to the Almighty, you will be restored... Surely then
you will find delight in the Almighty and will lift up your face to
God. You will pray to him, and he will hear you, and you will fulfill
your vows. What you decide on will be done, and light will shine
on your ways."*
-Job 22:23-28 [NIV]

On New Year's Eve in 2006, Tommy took me to downtown Atlanta to
watch the peach drop. Not only was I excited to be getting out of the
house, but it was always a thrill for me whenever he and I could spend
some quality time together. Before joining the crowds to ring in the new
year, we stopped at The Hard Rock Café for dinner. By this time, I had
observed a noticeable shift in Tommy's and Father's relationship, so I was
careful not to bring up Father unless Tommy did. Over dinner, Tommy
began to encourage me to go back to school and finish my degree. This
was the first time he had brought it up since I left the Christian university.
Wise beyond his years, Tommy was careful not to mention my degree
too soon. He waited several years after me leaving the university to bring
it back up because he knew I needed time to heal.

"Have you thought about returning and finishing your degree, Suzanne?" Tommy asked lovingly. By then, I had lost count of how many times Mother, Father, and Brother had each shoved this issue down my throat. Mother, who had never even attended college, continuously derided me for being a college dropout in between her lectures to "go back to school."

However, whenever Tommy mentioned something, I listened.

Much to his surprise, I answered with, "No, but it's not a bad idea," between gulps of Coke Zero. The look on his face and the sparkle in his eyes told me more than words ever could. He was proud of me.

It was too late to begin the upcoming semester, but by August 2007 I had officially transferred all my college credits from the previous university to a brand-new one. I was accepted and enrolled as a full-time student at Kennesaw State University.

I remember meeting a girl named Patricia in one of my 18th century English courses. She was from Pakistan, and (much to my surprise) she was also a devout Christian. In the middle of one of our group assignments, Patricia invited me to attend church with her. It's almost as if God handpicked Patricia to invite me to church because he knew I would never accept an invitation from what I would perceive to be a stereotypical, church-going Christian.

I felt something deep inside me that I had not felt in a long time. I felt a tug from God. I pondered her invitation for a moment, and then, I accepted.

Unfortunately, she came down with an unexpected cold and sent me a text message on Friday that she would not be able to attend church that Sunday. I stared at the message for a while, started typing a few different responses, and ended up not responding at all.

There goes that.

By the time Saturday came around, I could not stop thinking about her invitation. I surprised myself at how quickly I said "yes." I grew more curious and decided to look up her church online. Dayspring Church in Woodstock, GA. Woodstock! That was right by my school and not far from Mother and Father's house.

I felt something arise within me for the first time in longer than I could remember. I felt hope. What about Patricia, though? She was the only person I knew there, and she would not be there. Instantly, the story of Tommy's spontaneous Kwanzaa celebration at the Cobb EMC amphitheater came to my mind. At that moment, I wondered what Tommy would do in the situation. I almost called him up for advice, but it didn't take long for me to decide.

Patricia or no Patricia, I was going to church!

Before I knew it, Sunday morning had arrived, and I was off to church at a place where I knew not one soul. When Mother questioned where I was going, I spared myself the much-anticipated ridicule of going to church by myself and told her I was meeting my friend Patricia at church. She didn't need to know that Patricia wouldn't be there, and I wasn't about to be mocked for attending church alone. Mother did not respond but looked back to the television rerun of Judge Judy. I took that as my cue to leave.

I typed the address into my car's GPS, and before I knew it, I had arrived at my destination. Dayspring Church was a relatively small church building. It brought a giant smile to my face, thinking about how proud of me Tommy would be.

I stepped out of my black 1998 Camry, stood up straight, held my head up high, and walked inside.

Immediately, I was welcomed by so many warm faces. I knew all churches were required to have welcoming committees, but to my delight, they seemed genuine. How about that? I chuckled to myself.

After several more "hellos," I found a seat halfway to the back on the right of the semicircle-shaped auditorium. It was perfect. Not too close in case I needed to escape, but not too far away in case it was good.

As the worship band began, I couldn't help but notice a woman in the front row holding an adorable, rosy-cheeked little girl. That seriously had to have been the cutest toddler I have ever seen. She even raised her hands in worship! I sat back down after the band had played several worship songs and listened to the message. The head pastor was speaking about the story of Shadrach, Meshach, and Abednego in the fiery furnace. I listened to the story with amazement as I learned that Jesus saved the three from the deadly blazes because they were faithful to God and refused to bow down to King Nebuchadnezzar's golden statue. Once the pastor told the story, he reminded the congregation that the same God of Shadrach, Meshach, and Abednego is the same God we serve today, and God didn't save his miracles just for Biblical days—he does them today for you and me as well.

After the service, I couldn't help myself—I *had* to walk up to that woman and tell her how adorable her little girl was. "I'm sorry to bother you, but your little girl is so adorable," I said.

Like the rest of the people in her church, the woman was extremely kind and friendly. "My name's Jessica, and this is my daughter Naomi," she said.

"Naomi—what a beautiful name," I replied. Jessica and I instantly clicked. It was one of those times when you could tell you would end up being close friends with someone. We talked for so long that we were one of the last people to leave the building. Before I left, we exchanged phone numbers and became fast friends. I learned that she also was finishing her degree at Kennesaw State University. Not only were we friends, but we were also classmates.

And just like that, I had a friend who went to my church and school. Jessica was married to a man named Dave, they had two other children in addition to Naomi, and another one was on the way.

My friendship with Jessica became a lifesaver for me, as I often went to her home as an escape from mine. I would wake up in the morning to a text from her saying, "Coffee's on," and I knew I could just come over for the day.

During that time, I became extremely close with Jessica as well as the rest of her family. For the first time in my life, I thought to myself, *This is what family is supposed to feel like.* Nobody was yelling, dishes were not being thrown, and nobody was calling me a whore. Sign me up for this! It was also during this time that I discovered what it truly meant to be a Christian. Until then, I always thought Christianity was knowing a lot of Bible verses and being extremely pious.

I soon learned that Christianity was a *relationship*; a relationship with Jesus Christ, our Lord and savior. It was also at her house that I realized I had never truly accepted Christ into my heart as Lord and savior. I was ready. This inexplicable feeling of peace I received when I read the Bible or prayed—I wanted it, and I wanted it forever.

My best opportunity to truly learn about Jesus was during those days when I would drive over to Jessica's house and we would watch Andrew Wommack's Gospel Truth series. It was a set of twelve CDs, and Jessica and I would watch each and discuss the lesson afterward. Jessica and I talked about how peaceful and relaxing Andrew Wommack's voice was.

He wasn't like many of the colorful, charismatic evangelists I had seen while flipping channels on the TV. Some may even accuse Andrew of being dull, but Jessica and I saw him differently. We quickly learned that Andrew knew the truth. Because he was a living, breathing representation of the gospel of Jesus Christ—he didn't need an extravagant personality to make up for anything. The Word of God stands on its own. Andrew knew that people would recognize this, and those who accused him of being boring perhaps weren't at a place in their Christian walk to receive the plain, bonafide truth of the gospel of Jesus Christ.

I remember the moment when I flipped the script of my life. As I learned from Andrew Wommack and observed Jessica and her family, I told myself, "If this is Christianity, I want everything to do with it."

Jessica led me into a prayer one day at her home: "Lord, I recognize you as my Lord and savior. I believe that Jesus is the son of God and that he died and rose on the cross to save me from my sins. I ask you to please forgive me of my sins and come into my heart where you will forever be the Lord of my life. I pray these things in your son Jesus's precious name, amen."

After saying amen, Jessica hugged me and said, "Welcome to the family!" That was the day that my name was forever recorded in the Book of Life. Hallelujah!

Not long after accepting Christ into my life, I was water-baptized and then baptized in the Holy Spirit. I wanted so badly to find my prayer language, and I loved the Lord so much that I was determined to figure it out. Not long afterward, Jessica's family and I attended an Andrew Wommack Gospel Truth Seminar in downtown Atlanta. It was at the seminar where I received the book entitled *The New You and the Holy Spirit.* The book had a potter on the front molding a piece of clay—just like how the Lord molds the lives of his children.

I read in that book that, out of all people, Andrew also struggled to get his prayer language months after becoming a Christian and being baptized in the Holy Spirit. He said he finally received his breakthrough one day in the car, and some unknown syllables just came to him like any other language. He started by just repeating the one or two unknown syllables for about a week or two. After that, he began to learn more syllables, and it was only a matter of time before his prayer language became second nature to him.

Like Wommack, I started small with a few unknown syllables that rose in my spirit. Before long, I was adding to these syllables, and I could eventually begin praying in the Spirit without thinking about it.

I was, strangely, in Mother and Father's house when I officially received my prayer language. Elated, I called Jessica on the phone and exclaimed with utmost pride and joy, *"I sound Chinese!"*

It only took a moment for Jessica to figure out what in the world I was talking about. She was so happy for me, and I remember the phone conversation ending with her saying, *"Enjoy your Chinese!"*

I most certainly did!

February 20th, 2008,

How are you doing, my love? I recently watched an amazing music video made by Branch Church and the lyrics completely captivated my spirit. Of course, it instantly made me think of you. I am sharing the lyrics below. I look forward to hearing your sweet voice and our next dinner date.

With Eternal Love,
Uncle Tommy

"Creation Calls"

I have felt the wind blow whispering your name.
I have seen Your tears fall when I watch the rain.
How could I say there is no God, when all around creation calls?

A singing bird, a mighty tree. The vast expanse of open sea.
Gazing at a bird in flight, soaring through the air.
Lying down beneath the stars, I feel your presence there.

I love to stand at ocean's shore, and I feel the thundering breaker's roar.
To walk through golden fields of grain. 'Neath endless blue horizon's frame.

Listening to a river run, watering the earth.
Fragrance of a rose in bloom,, a newborn's cry at birth.

How could I say there is no God when all around creation calls?

Just like a child, I BELIEVE.
-Brian Doerksen

"Bless the days that saw us young, and the years that made us wise."
-Julia Ward Howe

Chapter Twenty-Eight
My College Graduation "Goal"

Before I knew it, college graduation was upon me: May 13th, 2008. I excitedly kept repeating the date in my mind. It's funny the things that stay in the mind as the years pass by. I always assumed that I would remember the shiny stage, the fabric of the gown, or the way the diploma felt clasped in my hands. Of course, I remember all of those beautiful things, but they are never the first memories that come to my mind.

The first memory that comes to my mind when I think of my college graduation was a date two months before—when I had been strong-armed into having breakfast with just Mother at The Waffle House. In those days, I was not exactly the string bean I used to be, but as I look upon pictures of that time in my late twenties, I often think to myself, *I wish I could go back to the size I was when I thought I was overweight.* Interestingly, once I had gained just a little meat on my bones, Mother's mockery of my weight shifted from name-calling to a more subtle (yet phony) sense of "encouragement" to lose weight.

As Mother and I sat on the benches with torn fabric listening to oldies' requests on the jukebox, I observed Mother take out one of her famous fashion magazines after putting in our order. Mother knew that it wouldn't be long until she was no longer able to mock me for being a college dropout. She needed to change her game. She was quiet for a bit, and I appreciated the silence. Suddenly, her hair—thin and dyed black—rose up from the fashion magazine. Sitting across from me, Mother slapped on yet another smile of synthetic encouragement, and her eyes lit up as much as they possibly could. Elated, she pointed her wrinkly finger to a bikini model, and—as if coming upon some profound sense of enlightenment—she blurted in the most inappropriate sugary-sweet tone, "Okay, now see, Suzanne, you can have your goal be to look like her by the time you graduate college."

Impossible. That woman needed a pork chop as much as I needed a loving Mother.

The remainder of the breakfast was quiet. Mother clanked down on her silverware, and I began silently regretting every bite of the order I placed and was now obliged to eat. Since I started school again full-time, Mother and Father had agreed to let me quit my job, so I no longer had to write them a monthly check for rent. So thoughtful. Since I did not have a job, I felt even more obligated to finish my meal because Mother had paid for it.

A few months passed, and it was time for me to walk the stage. Much to my surprise, Brother actually attended this graduation. Perhaps he felt remorse for not attending my miracle high school graduation. Of course, my beloved Uncle Tommy was there (as he always was for the big and little things in my life).

Pomp and Circumstance playing in the background, my gown—though indeed a cheap fabric—felt as if it were made completely of satin and I was a princess inside. I anxiously waited in the wings as the previous graduates received their accolades. Suddenly, it was time to call my name. I walked to the stage, almost mechanically, and it felt surreal—like a dream that was not happening. I was smiling, but it felt fake. I shook the Dean's hand, but it felt disingenuous. I smiled at the picture afterward, but something was missing.

As I cascaded back down the aisle holding my diploma, I kept asking myself, "Why am I feeling this way? I just graduated from college. I did the impossible—something I never thought I would achieve. I finally finished my degree! So why are these feelings erupting from my heart and mind?"

I remember looking up to the top level where Mother, Father, and Brother were seated. All faces were a blur except for Father's beaming face. I had not seen his face look like that in years.

Perhaps I was Daddy's little girl again.

Uncle Tommy was seated somewhere different—probably because he avoided Mother at all costs. I remember not needing to look up to find where he was sitting; Uncle Tommy was always with me. I did not need to look to the audience or anywhere else in this world for confirmation of that fact. Uncle Tommy was always in my heart and my spirit.

The brief moment of seeing the look on Father's face was a desired escape from my previous sense of disillusionment. I took my seat once again, but now as a college graduate. It did not take long for the same feeling of perplexity to return to my mind, clouding the joy I deserved to be feeling.

What was *wrong* with me? I had been so excited the entire year leading up to this moment, and now all I could feel was the sense that I was like a puppet being controlled by a marionettist. I remember it was not until the announcer came to the Y's that I received my revelation.

My college graduation had come, and I did not look like the bikini model on the front of that magazine. All I was thinking about that day was how much I let Mother down.

"Your beauty should not come from outward adornment, such as elaborate hairstyles and the wearing of gold jewelry or fine clothes. Rather, it should be that of your inner self, the unfolding beauty of a gentle and quiet spirit, which is of great worth in God's sight."
-1 Peter 3:3-4 (NIV)

May 13th, 2008,
My Dearest Suzanne,

Brother James still can't believe it… your Mother & Dad are still reeling in relief… But your good ole Uncle Tommy & Mimi are basking unabashed in your happiness. To the most beautiful English major to cross that stage! Congratulations, sweetheart!!!

I love you,
Uncle Tommy

Adulthood

Chapter Twenty-Nine
Nathan

My college graduation had come and gone, and until I found a job, I was still relegated to the confines of Mother's abusive walls. As a graduation present, Jessica gave me my first "grown-up" Bible. It was a New King James version, and she had "Suzanne" inscribed on the cover. On the inside, Jessica wrote: "May 13th, 2008—To Suzanne, I know God is going to do amazing things through you! Love, The Sprecher Family."

Just like that, my new Bible had become my most prized possession. My Bible and Jessica's house had become my two best means of escape from Mother's abuse. I read my Bible daily. There was something remarkable about how the pages shone on my face like the morning sunlight on a fresh rose. The word of God became my sustenance: my food, water, warmth, and shelter. It did not take long for me to identify my life verse: "Seek first the kingdom of God and all of its righteousness, and all these things shall be added unto you" (Matthew 6:33 [NKJV]).

During those days, I had fallen more and more in love with the Lord. So much so that I found myself focused on the first part of this verse (seek first the kingdom of God) without even thinking about the second part of the verse (all these things shall be added unto you). This verse would continuously prove true for the rest of my life. Whenever I focused on God first, His promise remained true: everything else would always fall perfectly into place (all these things were added unto me).

I thought about all of the failed relationships that ended in my heart being trampled on. I realized that God would never cheat on me. God would never stand me up. God would never dump me. My heart was finally safe with God, and I was not looking to give my heart to any human being ever again. Men weren't safe. God was.

I had finally forfeited my heart responsibly. I had given it to the maker of the universe, and for the first time in my life, I felt that love reciprocated.

Indeed, I was so head-over-heels in love with the Lord that I had resigned myself to becoming somewhat of a modern-day nun. When I shared my resolve with Jessica, she giggled and said, "Girl, you would get kicked out of a convent."

She probably wasn't wrong. Yet, I wanted it all. Whatever God wanted from me, I was ready to give.

Isn't it just like God to swoop in with the love of my life when I least expected it?

In my post-graduation days, I spent as much time over at Jessica's house as possible. Her family had become my family. I remember even going straight over to her house after my college graduation. I was still wearing my cap and gown, and I just wanted to hang out. Jessica was well aware of my dire need to escape the grips of Mother's "adult abuse," so it got to the point where she would let me stay at her house even when she was not there. She understood that I needed a safe place to go until I started working and got an apartment of my own.

When I wasn't looking for a job, I was reading my Bible, hanging out with Jessica, and going to church. I finally became an official member of Jessica's church and began serving as a nursery volunteer for the children's ministry. Back then, all you had to do was write down your name and phone number to show your genuine interest in working with children. These days, you go down to the police station, get fingerprinted for an FBI check, and furnish a police report to prove you are not a bank robber. I suppose, as a child abuse survivor, I am someone who can appreciate the child abuse checks (and all other checks, for that matter). I think it is sad to see how much things have changed since 2008.

Regarding my job search, I narrowed it down to one of two categories: technical writing or teaching English to elementary-aged children in Seoul, South Korea.

I remember applying to about a dozen technical writing jobs and being invited to several interviews. In the meantime, I kept one eye out for the possibility of overseas teaching. In those days, I had no other choice but to lie my head down under the same roof as Mother. I couldn't call Jessica at three A.M. when I needed shelter. I had to stay there, which quickly wore down the excitement of college graduation.

As a result of living under the roof of "adult abuse," the prospect of traveling seven thousand miles across the globe became more and more appealing with each passing day. In my mind, the further away I could get from the abuse, the better.

Less than two weeks after submitting my online application, I received a call from a recruiter for the position to teach English in South Korea. To my surprise, I had been accepted for the position, and they were looking to start the process to receive the proper documentation to move me forward. I accepted on the spot.

That same day, I received a text from Jessica. "Baby needs to be born early." I must have followed up with her in about ten messages, but it was evident that she was panicked and away from her cell. I rushed over to the hospital in my black Camry. By this time, she was in her third trimester, but it was still too disturbingly early to even think about her giving birth.

When I finally entered Jessica's room, the baby had been delivered and was in the NICU. You could feel the tension in the air. I was careful not to bring up the baby unless she did, and she did not. After a few moments, I started up a different conversation. "So, I was accepted for that teaching position in South Korea."

"You gonna go?"

"Yeah," I said. "I just need to get away from all of this for a while."

"That's understandable," Jessica replied.

At that moment, a mutual friend, Tanya, entered the door. Jessica and I both knew Tanya from church, and she was a naturally gifted encourager—the type of person you genuinely enjoy being around. She could uplift the most downtrodden and depressed with inspiration and hope within a single conversation.

Oh good, Tanya's here. She'll know exactly what to say, I thought to myself.

To no surprise, Tanya had something profound to say—only it wasn't to Jessica. It was to me.

Stoic, Tanya looked me straight in the eye and said, "I'm going to pray for you to get a job." I quickly answered her, "Oh, don't even worry about it—I was just telling Jessica about how I accepted an offer to teach English to elementary students in South Korea."

"No, I'm going to pray for you to get another job," Tanya replied. Though it was a little strange, I just smiled and did not give it much thought.

Until the next day came.

I was in the Target parking lot, and I was just about to get into my car when an unknown number called. I let it ring several times and then picked up, "Hi, this is Suzanne!"

Soon, I would realize that the gentleman on the other line was my future boss of five years at an engineering firm where I would be working. It was also the place where I met my future husband and the love of my life. It made no sense to accept the job offer at the time, because that meant living with the abuse for a bit longer.

I did it anyway.

I went against all reason and listened to the still, small voice within me. Pulling me—beckoning me to stay.

I had enough money saved in my account to live in an extended-stay motel for the first week of my new job as a technical writer. Right before my start date, one of Mother's most vicious terror attacks broke out. It happened when I told her about the job offer that I had accepted. Perhaps her turmoil came from the fact that she knew I would once again be free from the confines of her abusive grip.

I knew I had to be in a different environment for at least the first week of my new job. There's no way I would have kept that job if I came in looking like a toad from crying every morning when I first started. The extended-stay motel was the perfect escape.

It's funny, looking back on things now. The day I met my husband, I was secretly living in an extended-stay motel. Every day during the first week of my new job, I would leave the motel (which was less than ten minutes away from my office) and I would drive to work just like every other employee there. Nobody needed to know that I was coming from an extended-stay motel, and I surely would not tell them. I certainly was not going to tell my cute new coworker and future husband Nathan about it! When it was time to go "home," I just got in my car and drove to the extended-stay motel for the night. I repeated this pattern for the first week, and it worked in my favor.

Nathan was everything I ever longed for in a husband, but had given up in trying to attain. I still cannot decide what attracted me to him most, his patience, his sense of humor, his gentleness, his kindness, or most importantly his love for the Lord.

I knew that by the time I had to actually go home, things would be safer in Mother and Father's house. You see, the longer I ran away or disappeared, the better things were when I got home. Mother just kept things mildly unpleasant until it was time for another round. At this rate, I could stay in Mother and Father's house for just enough time to save up for a down payment on an apartment before the next terror attack. In just two weeks, I had the money secured, and I was forever free from the imprisoning confines of that house.

"Look in the scroll of the LORD and read: None of these will be missing, not one will lack her mate. For it is his mouth that has given the order, and his Spirit will gather them together.
-Isaiah 35:16 (NIV)

Chapter Thirty

The Sabotage Attempt

Sometimes, God changes the trajectory of our lives in a way that fits his plan for us. Not only was I stopped from leaving the country to meet Nathan, but he was also on his way out of Georgia the day we met. For the past couple of months, a similar position within the same company had been courting him. The position was attractive at the time for Nathan not so much because it was in Kansas, but because more of his friends in the company lived in Kansas.

In just two weeks, I learned from a coworker that Nathan had turned down a job offer in Kansas. This was the first time I had even heard about the job offer. At this point, he and I had been secretly dating for a while. We already knew we loved each other; what we didn't know was if the company allowed employees to love each other or not. So we did our best to keep it a secret, but we were sure everybody knew anyway.

When my coworker informed me of the news, I pulled her aside and said, "What job? He was offered a new job?"

With a twinkle in her eye, she replied, "He used to want it before he met you," and she walked out of my office with a smile.

I remember smiling so big on the inside that it had to have shown on the outside. *He loves me.*

Sometimes, God works miracles that are so inexpressibly mysterious you cannot help but fall more and more in love with him.

Fall has been my favorite season since meeting Nathan. It's the season indelibly marked in my memory as the time when I fell in love with Nathan. I remember we had each said we loved each other by October. We were falling and falling fast. It was only a matter of time before he popped the big question.

Nathan, being the respectful gentleman he was, decided to go the traditional route and take Mother and Father out for dinner to ask for my Father's permission to marry me.

Watch out for Mother, Nathan. Hopefully she wouldn't hurl any bread rolls at his head and shout, "Why didn't you ask me, too?"

Fortunately for my future fiance, he received Father's blessing with no bread rolls flying in the air. He recounted that Mother had the stupidest look on her face at the time, like somebody had just asked her what the color orange smelled like.

Most non-abusive parents keep things like this a secret, as most proposals are planned surprises. However, Mother was losing me; she was losing me quickly, and she had to do something.

My soon-to-be-fiance returned home, and I was shocked to hear that it went smoothly. I kept waiting for the other shoe to drop. It usually never took long.

Sure enough, less than ten minutes passed by when I heard the resounding ding on my phone, indicating that I had one unread text message.

This couldn't be good. I knew it was Mother. Sure enough, as I raised the phone to my eyes and read the screen, I gazed upon the following words:

"CONGRATULATIONS, SUZANNE!!! I knew you guys would get married! XOXO Mom & Dad."

I knew what she was trying to do. She was trying to sabotage Nathan's proposal. Fortunately for us, her plan completely backfired. She didn't realize how poorly my beau and I kept secrets from each other. We were the worst, but always with the best of intentions. Nathan would go buy me a necklace, and before he could give it to me, he would spill the beans. Likewise, I would try my best to surprise him with a nice meal or a thoughtful gift, and each time the secret left my lips far in advance because I was just too excited to keep it from him.

"Woe to those who call evil good and good evil, who put darkness for light and light for darkness, who put bitter for sweet and sweet for bitter.
-Isaiah 5:20 (NIV)

It was hard to keep such deep joy a secret from each other. As expected, the proposal followed suit, and I already knew what he was doing that night in addition to the question he soon planned to ask.

Mother was none the wiser on any of this, and she had thought her text message crushed the joy and surprise of his proposal. In her mind, she was winning.

 I felt sorry for her.

The big night came, and even though we both knew what was planned that evening well before Mother's intended sabotage, it did not drain an ounce of excitement from the situation. He was going to propose to me! We were going to get married!

Although I knew the purpose of the evening, my darling boyfriend kept many of the specific details of the night from me. I did not know where we were going, nor how he would do it. Sometimes, when things seem to be falling apart, they work out perfectly. Such was the case for my and my beloved's proposal. When we finally arrived at the mystery destination, I saw it was Stone Mountain. He had planned to take me to the Christmas Lights festival, get down on one knee, and propose amid the festivities. We soon found out that the place was closed. On top of that, it was starting to drizzle a bit. Nathan saw discouragement; I saw an opportunity. Defeated, Nathan was about to cancel when I asked the gentleman at the gate if we could drive through anyway. Much to our surprise, he agreed, and the next thing we knew, we were on a private tour of the Stone Mountain Park lights—just the two of us.

It was perfect.

Not much time had passed when we stopped by an extra-high Christmas tree adorned with light green and white lights. The rain was falling lightly upon our heads. As we stood by the Christmas tree that night, my beloved knelt and asked me to be his wife right there in front of that lit-up pine.

It was the best night of my life. After all, I was going to be marrying the love of my life.

January 29th, 2010,
My Dearest Suzanne,

Congratulations to my blue-eyed wonder!!! My baby Suzanne is getting married!!! It seems surreal to me, like it was yesterday that I was holding you for the first time. There is a part of me that will now never be the same now that you are no longer a little girl anymore, but I could not be happier for you. Nathan is a good man—you married well, love. I have nothing to worry about anymore. You are going to be okay. Cheers to the lovely bride and groom! I'll be there with bells on!!!

With Deep Love,
Uncle Tommy

"GRACE"

The friend of age
And guide of youth.
Few hearts like his
With virtue warm'd.
Few heads with
Knowledge so informed.
If there's another world,
He lives in Bliss,
If there is none…
He made the most of this.

-Robert Burns

Planning & The Big Day

Nathan and I lost track of how many times we were tempted to go to Vegas and elope throughout the tumultuous ups and downs of planning our big day. At a certain point, it became humorous that my and Nathan's names were even on the wedding invitations. It felt more appropriate for guests to receive:

"It's Mother's big day! Come watch the thing she made (Suzanne) get married, and note all the details!"

We were trapped in months of meetings, appointments, screaming fights, and more meetings. She had started the dress shopping with a warning: "Whatever you do, Suzanne, do not go to David's Bridal." Not that I wanted to go to David's Bridal, but it seriously annoyed me that she gave me no choice in the matter, so I chose to go there anyway just to get under her skin.

I'll never forget the evening that I finally selected my wedding dress. Mother had no emotion as I donned my beautiful wedding gown. She was so emotionless and out of sync with me that we both had to look to some girl's dad to confirm it was the one. A stranger had caught on to the occasion of finding my wedding dress, but not my Mother.

One thing I had going for me was that since it was only a bridal shop and not a large strip mall, Mother could not abandon me without a ride home. Just kidding—she left me on the side of Barrett Parkway in Kennesaw, Georgia the night I got my wedding dress. Memories.

Fortunately, I was no longer eight years old and I owned a cell phone—no walking home for five miles for me. My knight in shining armor, Nathan, came and picked me up on the side of the road. I just got into his car like it was no big deal because, after all, it had become sort of a twisted family tradition.

"Hey babe, I got my wedding dress!" I exclaimed.

"Okay…" Nathan replied as he slowly started to get a taste of what I had grown up with.

It's almost as if Uncle Tommy had a sixth sense when it came to me. He always called or wrote when I needed him the most. The card that surrounded this following letter was probably one of my favorites. It was a tightrope performer flying in the air amid Mother's lofty wedding. He was there to enjoy himself! It was like Hunting Island all over again!

April 16th, 2010,
Baby Girl!

Have you come up for air yet from planning your mother's wedding? Haha! Don't get mad at me—you know I'll make it all about you despite what she wants! As we enter the days leading up to your wedding day, I think of Hunting Island and how you have always marched to the beat of your own drum, Suzanne. Never lose that unique creativity! It will serve you well in life! I am signing off now. Not too much longer and you'll be walking down that aisle, a beautiful bride.

All My Love Under the Sun,
Uncle Tommy

On my wedding day, I remember Mother looked like a deer in headlights in the dressing room area where all the girls were getting ready. I guess she was nervous. I scanned her for any trace of emotion. No sign of life. She was trying to change up the plans last-minute for how Nathan was to retrieve my garter at the reception. "It's not lady-like for him to reach up your dress like that."

I ignored her.

Finally, the big moment was upon me. Father was standing in the lobby dressed to the nines. Perhaps he looked that lovely for me—not for Mother. He motioned to me to say something, and I turned my ear towards him. *Maybe he'll tell me something sweet, or say I'll always be his little girl.* I listened in anticipation.

"Now remember, you stand in front of the minister, and I'm to the left of him," he said, rehearsing something we practiced the night before. At this point in his life, it was the most profound emotion he could give to me. It's almost as if Mother had sucked all of the loving Father out of him. I knew he wanted to say something more profound and memorable deep down.

"Okay," I said in an understanding voice. I knew he was trying—it was just all gone.

Walking down the aisle was a blur for me. A transition from Mother's daughter to Nathan's wife. It was long overdue. I was legally free to no longer go by my last name, and I got rid of it immediately. A couple of solos were sung, and then came Tommy's scripture reading.

To this day, my husband and I will always hear the sound of his words at our wedding whenever we think of good ole Uncle Tommy.

"Love is patient, love is kind. It does not envy, it does not boast, it is not proud. It does not dishonor others, it is not self-seeking, it is not easily angered, it keeps no record of wrongs. Love does not delight in evil but rejoices with the truth. It always protects, always trusts, always hopes, always perseveres. Love never fails… And now these three remain: faith, hope, and love. But the greatest of these is love."
-1 Corinthians 13:4-13 [NIV]

August 21st, 2010,
My Dearest Suzanne,

My little girl is married and all grown up. I am so happy for you and cannot wait to catch up with you after the honeymoon!

Forever Yours,
Uncle Tommy

"They May Not Need Me,
Yet , They Might! I'll Let My Head
Be Just in Sight.
A Smile As Small As Mine
Might Be,
Precisely, Their Necessity."

-Emily Dickenson

The Great Awakening

June 6th, 2013 was a monumental day in my life; it was the day I became a mother. I had been in labor for seventeen and a half 17 ½ hours and was fully dilated. Nathan stepped into the restroom for a moment, and during the time he had left the room, my and my baby's heart rate suddenly started dropping. Nathan returned from the bathroom to a room full of men and women in blue scrubs shouting stern, unfamiliar medical terminology.

Within what seemed like one second, a form was shoved in my face for me to sign and I was forced to chug a very thick, dark liquid. Everything was a daze. The doctor yelled, "Get this room prepped, stat!" Stat. Now, I was no medical doctor, but I had seen enough episodes of Grey's Anatomy to know that "stat" was not good.

My condition was so severe that they did not allow Nathan in the operating room with me until mine and the baby's vitals were stabilized. It was the scariest four minutes of my entire life. I almost died giving birth. I believe Nathan's required absence from the room was even worse than my current physical condition. Everything was always okay as long as I had my beloved by my side.

After an eternity, my groom could finally join me in the operating room. Moments later, we would both hear the most intensifying, magical shrill: the sound of our newborn baby's first cry.

It was the best sound I had ever heard, and nothing else mattered anymore except the arrival of this new life.

I remember my recovery taking longer than I expected, but I was ready to hold my newborn baby. The moment I held him, I felt Heaven in my arms and the glory of the Lord amid the chaos. I remember seeing that my son had Nathan's nose at first (which is funny because now that he has grown up, he has my nose). I saw love.

The hospital kept me overnight for the next few days while I recovered from the emergency cesarean section. It did not take long after Luke's magnificent entrance into the world for me to pick up on some subtle, alarming messages from The Holy Spirit.

I don't remember if it was the second or the third time I saw my new baby. All I remember was that it was not the very first time, but one of the first times I had laid eyes on him. An unfamiliar feeling came upon my whole being. I remember thinking, "What is wrong with me? Why am I not elated right now"? I wasn't feeling all the warm fuzzies I was supposed to. No, I was disturbed.

It was not until I gazed upon the innocent face of my precious newborn baby that the facts hit me cold in the face: I had been abused.

It's funny how some words are so taboo. Abuse. Rape. Murder. I'm willing to bet those who have committed such acts are hesitant to label their behavior correctly. That was the case for Mother. It was always, "She's crazy, but she loves me." It wasn't until I had a child that I realized, *Oh my God, she didn't love me. Oh my God, I was abused.* I thought about all my experiences with Mother. As I looked at my precious newborn, suddenly, those things were officially without excuse. I could never imagine leaving this precious child on the side of the road, abandoning him in busy shopping malls, or letting him run away for days without even bothering to look for him.

It wasn't long until yet another life-altering revelation came upon me. Chills scurried down the hairs of my neck and arms as I suddenly thought, *This was how Mother felt when I was born.*

"When I was a child, I talked like a child, I thought like a child, I reasoned like a child. When I became a [wo]man, I put the ways of childhood behind me."
-1 Corinthians 13:11

May 24th, 2013,

Happy happy birthday my beloved Suzanne! I keep wanting to say "Baby Suzanne," but perhaps "Having-A-Baby Suzanne" is now more appropriate!

You will always be my Baby Suzanne, no matter your age.

Love,
Uncle Tommy

Letting Go

Realizing I had been abused as a child was a significant breakthrough in my life. I would later learn in therapy that there was a name for Mother's condition. She was not just "crazy." Mother suffered from narcissistic personality disorder (NPD). There's something incredibly liberating about putting a name to a condition or experience—labeling it, filing it away in the wrinkles of the mind. It justified things for me. Ironically, I felt less crazy the more I understood that she was more than just crazy; it was clinical and legitimized.

Perhaps one of the most therapeutic (yet hurtful) parts of my time in therapy was to realize the worst possible fact a child could imagine: *My mother did not love me.* I'll repeat it for those in the back: *My mother did not love me.*

I know that, technically, it was not her fault, and to this day the only thing I genuinely blame her for is just not getting help. After a lifetime of abuse, there's only one thing I hold her responsible for. Still, I could not deny the primal ache I felt from not being loved by my mother.

I read half a library full of books on NPD. To glance at my bookshelf in those days, one would think that I was either a psychiatrist or studying to become one. I might as well have been. Despite the volumes of academic knowledge I obtained on the subject, I still had the ache to contend with. I was desperate to find some closure.

In a final act of desperation, I went to a local toy store and bought a small bag of pink helium balloons. When I got home, I blew one of them up and taped a piece of paper on the side. The writing on the paper was blunt and finite: *My mother should have loved me.* Afterward, I stepped out onto our back deck and stood at the railing for an eternity.

I have to let go. I have to let go….

Standing on the edge of my back patio, I contemplated the words Uncle Tommy spoke at my wedding.

"Love is patient, love is kind. It does not envy, it does not boast, it is not proud. It does not dishonor others, it is not self-seeking, it is not easily angered. It keeps no record of wrongs. Love does not delight in evil, but rejoices with the truth. It always protects, always trusts, always hopes, always perseveres."
-(1 Corinthians 13:4-7)

As I pondered these words on the true meaning of love, it helped me come to terms with the harsh reality that what I experienced with Mother was *not* love. I can feel and think as much as I want, but when I measure my life against the word of God, there is a certainty that man cannot achieve. This scripture helped me to finally let go.

The moment arrived when I felt the curled, white ribbon slowly slip from the clenched grasp of my fingers. In the blink of an eye, the balloon wildly escaped into the air and ascended to the Heavens above. I was not comfortable with how fast it was traveling away from my sight. It was leaving forever. As the image above me slowly transformed from a balloon to a small circle and then a minuscule dot, my hopes of ever having an earthly mother to love me went along with it. Eventually, the pink dot completely disappeared into an unmistakable blue canvas sky. I had to come to terms with the fact that it was gone forever.

Hunting Island Flashback: Still the Same Free Spirit

May 24th, 2015,
Happy Birthday to my beloved Suzanne!

Ah, the times—they are changing! All available adult energies are now devoted to our young. When one reaches fifty, the birthday gong resounds! So share the joy & youthful laughter while you can.

"The sands of time grind slowly… but, they grind exceedingly well."

Hoping all is well in meaningful abundance at the Ostrander household. Hugs to you & Sir Luke! Greetings to Nathan, too!

All My Love,
Uncle Tommy

Chapter Thirty-Four
The Final Escape

Although I had peacefully come to terms with letting go of the hope of having a mother to love on this Earth, the following months dragged by with a perpetual sense of dread as I relived the moment when I gazed upon my innocent newborn son in the hospital and knew I had been abused. Abused. I had been. I had. I, abused. I had been abused. The words scrambled themselves as they echoed throughout the innermost cavities of my mind, and it did not take long to figure out that something major—something significant—had to happen for this sense of dread to go away.

By that point, I had read enough books on NPD and abuse to register the fact that this was a profoundly deep generational pattern that was not just going to go away on its own. It was that knowledge alone that perhaps terrified me the most. What was I going to do? I refused to end up like Mother.

I became increasingly angry at Mother in those days—knowing that she had felt the same thing when I was born (as her Mother had abused her) but not doing anything about it. How could she ignore this dreadful reality? Who does that? Was it just that a monumental change of that caliber would have been inconvenient for her?

Convenience. The abuse was what she knew. It was all that she knew. She would have to start all over and reconstruct her understanding of selfless love and parenting. So much change. It's too bad my future was not worth it for her. My future stood on the precipice of convenience. She continued the cycle because she chose the path of least resistance. I was not worth the journey of the road less traveled.

Despite the myriad of uncertainties in my mind during those days, there was one thing I knew for sure: My baby was worth the sacrifice to stop the cycle. I had made up my mind that I would do whatever it took—even if it killed me—to make sure I did not become a child abuser.

I knew I had to do something big; it just took a while for me to realize what that big thing was. A few weeks passed, and I became more haunted by this revelation. Big. Something big. I scanned my mind for any other feelings that might help lead me in the right direction of this "something big." Suddenly, I found traces of the thought, *We have to get out.* I clung to that thought as if my life depended on it, and perhaps it did. Out. We have to get out. Have to get out. I knew we had to get out, but what did that mean? I finally realized that I was making things much more complicated than they needed to be. "We have to get out" meant just the way it sounded. Simply put, we had to move away. Far away.

Luke was around eighteen months old. I had been training for my first half-marathon in Atlanta. I resigned to becoming fully dedicated to helping Nathan find a job closer to his family in the Midwest. I finished my first half-marathon in March 2015 with a time of two hours and seventeen minutes. Now, my next marathon was ahead of me: getting our family out.

To my surprise, it only took only two months to find Nathan a job in Pittsburgh. The previous Christmas, we were shopping in Pittsburgh while visiting his family. Right in the middle of that mall, we just decided, "Let's live here." The process of finding Nathan a job was relatively seamless. He would go to work during the day, and each day (when Luke napped), I would get online and apply to as many electrical engineering jobs in Pittsburgh as possible. Two months wasn't very long to find and secure a new job to move my family away.

I remember the day Nathan's job offer came in. It was the first week in May. In just two weeks, we put our house on the market, sold our home, and arranged to live with Nathan's family in Ohio while we looked for a new house in Pittsburgh.

"God is faithful, and he will not let you be tempted beyond your ability, but with the temptation he will also provide the way of escape, that you may be able to endure it."
-1 Corinthians 10:13 (ESV)

On May 21st, 2015, Nathan, Luke, and I packed our things and drove away from Georgia forever. It felt as if we were driving away into the sunset that day. It marked the last time I ever ran away. This time, I stayed away.

Chapter Thirty-Five
A Safe Haven

"My people will live in peaceful dwelling places, in secure homes, in undisturbed places of rest."
-Isaiah 32:18 (NIV)

Before leaving town, Nathan and I had secured a storage unit in Western Pennsylvania. In two weeks, Nathan would come back down to Georgia and close on our house and help the movers pack up the remains of our home. Our first stop was Nathan's parents' house in Ohio. His parents let us stay with them as we were selling our house and looking for a new one in Pennsylvania. Nathan had a bit of a commute from Ohio to his new job in Pennsylvania every day, but it was worth it for us to relocate and live in peace.

The minute I stepped into the front door of Nathan's parents' house, I felt a pleasant yet unfamiliar sense of order, love, and serenity. This must have been what it was like for him growing up. I slowly began to understand that Nathan and his sister had been loved.

The house was safe. I imagine Nathan never had to duck to avoid objects flying towards his head at this home. The carpet was clean. I imagine there was never any shampoo or blood emptied onto it. Then, of course, there was the bathtub. As I looked at their bathtub, I knew that nobody had almost frozen to death in it. It was just a normal tub used for bathing. How delightfully odd. It was almost as if nobody had ever been abused in this home. Could this home be real?

The house had crocheted pillows about what it was like to be a mom. I had never been in such a loving environment in my entire lifetime.

Loving pictures of family adorned the walls of the hallway. You could tell how proud the parents were of the children. You could almost say that family was the decorative theme. It was new. It was crisp. There were no demons of abuse present in that home. Outside of boarding school, it was the first time I felt like I was in a safe, nurturing environment. It would be easy for me to resent Nathan for being born into a non-abusive family, but I do not, nor do I resent anyone born into a loving family. I'm truly happy for those who have been loved the right way. Why would I ever wish my own experience on anyone else?

If there's anything about moving to the Midwest that I remember, it is the uncanny sense of relief I felt when I looked at my little boy. Finally, I could breathe. I felt an overwhelming wave of peace telling me that everything would be all right. I had the freedom to love my son the way a mother is supposed to love a child. The moment I knew everything was going to be okay, it also registered to me that Mother had never felt this feeling her entire life. She stayed trapped in her own prison, never knowing what it was like to truly be free. For that, I felt only the utmost compassion for her.

July 28th, 2015
Suzanne, Nathan, and Sir Luke!

Greetings from the Hot Box Atlanta! It's over 95 degrees every day, dispelled momentarily by late afternoon showers—autumn will not come soon enough!

So, how are you three faring in the Midwest? Suzanne, I know your father misses you, but I also am keenly aware as described to me in a very loving letter from our Mimi that Suzanne is a "free spirit." And this rare human species needs space to stretch out, explore, and enjoy life to the fullest. So, she knows well and smiles down approvingly. You will thrive as you find your way. And, while Luke naps away, don't forget that creative mind between your ears. You have the gift of creative writing—use it and never lose it!

I hope James finds his way. He says he is much dissatisfied as an insurance underwriter. I hope he finds a way to a career to stimulate him.

I will miss Nathan this year at our annual golf tournament. We have thirty-six golfers signed on for this fall. I assume Nathan will not be able to attend. We especially like it when former champions make the pilgrimage. I will miss his good presence.

Make the most of your new environment. A new culture, a different game… from go Dawgs to go Bearcats and sometimes go Buckeyes!

Much Love From Down Yonder!
Uncle Tommy

Cycle-Breaker

I remember the night; clear skies amongst a deep, blue lagoon.
We finally did it, kid:
We lassoed the moon.
-CO

"Violence shall no more be heard in your land, devastation or
destruction within your borders; you shall call your walls Salvation,
and your gates Praise."
-Isaiah 60:18 (NIV)

It has been said to never underestimate a cycle-breaker. Not only did they face years of generational abuse, but they looked the pain straight in the eye and said, "This stops with me." This comes at a significant cost. Never underestimate a cycle-breaker.

I broke the cycle.

In August 2015, Nathan, Luke, and I closed on our home in Pennsylvania. It was close to Nathan's new job in a mysterious land called Moon

Township. It might as well have been on the moon since we knew no soul there. None of that mattered to me, though. We finally had a home of our own in Pennsylvania, and we were away from the fire and the storm in Georgia. We were safe, and we had a place to call home.

The pictures below are of me, my husband Nathan, our oldest son Luke, and our youngest son Levi (born

in Pennsylvania in 2020). Being a cycle-breaker of child abuse, I believe, is perhaps my most significant life accomplishment.

May 24th, 2017

Happy of happiest birthdays to my daughter of deep blue skies. I think of you all of the time. Hope all is well in the household.

Unconditional Love Across the Miles,

Good 'Ole Uncle Tommy

Chapter Thirty-Seven

The Agenda Part I

"All a person's ways seem pure to them, but the motives are weighed by the LORD."
-Proverbs 16:2 (NIV)

In 2018, my daddy was finally coming to Pennsylvania to visit his little girl. I spent weeks in an air of excitement, imagining finally returning to the days when it was just the two of us against the world. He would finally love me again. There would be no strings attached….

We arrived at the Pittsburgh International Airport to pick up my dad. From afar, I was the first to immediately spot his long, gray sportcoat and wool hat. *That's my daddy!*

We had a wonderful time during his stay with us. He and I went on walks. We took Luke to a movie and walked around the shopping malls afterward. *It was just like the good old days.*

I suppose I was far too smitten with joy to be even remotely prepared for what would happen next.

The other shoe dropped.

On the last night of his visit, he strategically waited for a moment when Nathan was in another room and ambushed me to bring Mother back into my life.

It was supposed to have just been Daddy and I like old times. It was then that I realized the days of no strings attached were forever gone. I thought he had come up to see me; I thought he had wanted to spend time with me—to reconnect with his only living daughter.

Boy, was I fooled. He had an agenda for this entire trip. When he bought his plane ticket, he thought about Mother, not me. As he greeted me in the airport for the first time in years, he thought about Mother, not me. His entire trip was a greasy campaign to bring my abuser back into my life.

Make no mistake, the joke was absolutely on me.

January 26th, 2018

Dear Uncle Tommy,

I hope this letter finds you well. I just wanted to send you a quick note to say hello and send some love your way down in Georgia. How have you been? It feels like the more distance between us, the closer we become.

Speaking of which, I wanted to confide in you about something. My dad came up for a visit last month, and everything seemed magical. We spent quality time together, he bonded with Luke, and everything seemed perfect until the last day of his visit.

On his last day here, he waited for a moment when Nathan was not around and basically ambushed me to bring my mother back into my life.

I felt angry, foolish, and profoundly sad at this revelation. It made me question the intent behind the entire trip. I thought he genuinely wanted to spend time with me. He purposely waited for the last day to bombshell me because he knew it would upset me.

Looking back on what I hoped would be tender memories of our time together, I now see not Daddy and I but Mother hovering in the corner, forever engrafted in each memory.

What should I do?

Your Loving Goddaughter,
Suzanne.

February 20th, 2018,
My Dearest Suzanne,

Ambushed to bring back your mother… I can only imagine what that must have been like. Whatever happened, I am sorry everyone cannot discern reality. If it is to be, it will be in its own time and place. Such emotional tensions are anything but programmable on demand!

In the end, all will be well. Of this, I am most certain. I will invite him to an upcoming Civil War lecture, and afterward, we will spend some time together to discuss this. Believe me, I've got your best interest at heart, so don't go there with saying "I don't want to be a bother or a nuisance." I know what things are like for you because I know you care so much. Look at how much you care for Nathan and little Luke.

Speaking much on behalf of Mimi, we had many talks throughout her lifetime—especially about you, Suzanne. You were the brilliant shining light, the creative writer, the free spirit, always bouncing around. You were a shining light—and that's why we both love you. We both agreed on the concern that your creative spirit might be curtailed and short-circuited under the yoke of your mother. I promised her I would look after you, which I intend to do.

Along with me, Mimi is beaming with joy at her dearly beloved granddaughter's continuing journey through uninterrupted, uncorrupted, creative genius!

YOU GO GIRL!!!

Love, As All Ways & Always,
Uncle Tommy

"Say yes when nobody asks."
-Lao Proverb

Chapter Thirty-Eight
The Mediator

"Blessed are the peacemakers, for they will be called children of God."
-Matthew 5:9 (NIV)

July 16th, 2018
My Dearest Suzanne,

Well… it finally happened! I met with your good old dad, and we had a fulfilling time together discussing our dearly beloved Suzanne.

To begin with, I have known your mother for many many August moons. She remains a study in confusion. The fact that she decided to keep secret that your mom and your dad had both experienced failed marriages remains a mystery to me, even to this day.

Understand that your father is not wired like you or me. It is the Great Commission that makes each of us who we are. It is the exact reason you and I are, and will remain, a closer bond than me and your brother and, honestly, even me and your good dad. Your father is a decent human. I am at a loss of words with him other than he just "doesn't get it." It's all a matter of perspective, and his is quite clearly entangled in your mother's and has been for many years. A close friend once described me as a most spiritual person. One could never say that about either your father, your brother, or especially your mother. Suzanne, we should have been brother and sister. We would have, together, jumped into the surf at Hunting Island, even after your mother told us not to! That is how we are wired. I am helpless to assist you in seeing that very light, which is soooo evident to me.

I wish you had the time and the opportunity to know Mimi as closely as I did. You were only eleven when she passed away and asked me to watch over you. Mimi knew all along you were wired differently from your entire family. So it was no surprise to me when she asked me to please shield you from those short-circuited family ties that would possibly curtail your incredibly creative makeup. I can only tell the tale. Once she verbalized her request, I knew exactly where she was coming from. The fact that she much adored her granddaughter, Sweet Suzanne, is an understatement of gigantic proportions. Mimi always worried about you. Much of that anxiety came from knowing how very different you were from both to your mother and brother. She only wanted to see you bloom!!! She was keen to conjure how life at home could easily stifle your immaculately creative imagination.

I will write more later. Ta-ta and all my love till next we meet.

Forever, Fervently Your Biggest Fan,
Uncle Tommy

Chapter Thirty-Nine

The Agenda Part II

A year had come and gone since Father's campaign visit. Like the leaves that fell to the ground upon schedule, Father reached back out to me around the same time to schedule his annual visit. *Okay...* I thought to myself. *This time will be different. The first time was just a flop; this time, it will just be him and I against the world; this time, it will be how I wanted it to be: I will be Daddy's little girl again, just like old times. This time will be different.*

Like the year before, Nathan, Luke, and I met Father at the Pittsburgh International Airport, and I was excited about his visit. This time around was extra special because I had an exclusive art show coming up during his stay. Since his last trip, I had started a small business selling handcrafted knitted items (scarves, hats, gloves, baby blankets, stuffed animals, etc.). I knew I needed a sophisticated name—something classy that truly spoke to my character: The Knit Wit. Sometimes, when you know, you know.

Just like the first, Father's second visit was jam-packed with many fun activities. From going to the movies with Luke to window shopping at the local mall to a trip to the pumpkin patch, we did it all. On his second to last day here, he worked the art booth with me for my craft show. When Mother heard I was starting to sell my knitted items, she stiffly said, "Bless her heart." Apparently, I was to be pitied. Unlike Mother, Father was excited about the new company and did not seem to share her apparent sympathy for the venture. The night before the craft show, he stayed up late with me, helping me stuff bags and assigning the proper price tags to items. This trip was going entirely differently—I could feel it. I was that much closer to becoming "Daddy's little girl."

The craft show came and went and was a roaring success—except for the adorable moose I made. Actually, he was a reindeer, but perhaps he identified as a moose because people kept saying, "How much for the moose?" and I eventually stopped correcting them. Either way, the reindeer who identified as a moose did not sell.

The next day came, and it was Father's last day here. He and I went on a walk and talked about all sorts of things. None of the topics included Mother. It was like my dream was coming true. I guess I finally had him back for good this time.

Just before nightfall, Nathan, Luke, Father, and I were busy tying loose ends around the house before we left to drive Father back to the airport. This had been the best trip yet. We reached the airport and got to security. I walked Father up, and Nathan stayed behind with Luke. I gave Father a delighted hug and told him how much fun I had with him and to text me when he landed. Father then turned to me and spoke words that my eardrums wanted no part in receiving.

"I think it's time to bring your Mother back into your life, honey. It's been a long time."

I ended the hug and just looked at him with disappointed eyes. The joke, once again, was on me. It had all been a setup. How could I have been so stupid not to see through this solid agenda? Why did I imagine things would just be the two of us this time? It was then and there that I realized it would never again just be Daddy and me. I had forever lost him to Mother.

As I watched him remove his shoes and place his bag on the conveyor belt, I knew it would be the last time I would ever see him.

*"Though my mother **and** father forsake me, the Lord will receive me."*
-Psalm 27:10 (NIV)

December 13th, 2018
Dear Uncle Tommy,

Hello! How have you been? It's been a minute since I've written, so I thought that you should hear from me that Father and I are on a very, very long—if not indefinite—break. He came up again, and the same exact thing happened: He waited for a moment when Nathan was not around, and right before he left, he ambushed me to bring Mother back into my life. There's nothing neither you nor I can do at this point, as I feel we have both tried everything. God bless you, Godfather, for being the peacemaker that you are. I'm so sorry that things did not turn out the way you and I had hoped they would.

I will love you as long as forever.

Your Goddaughter,
Suzanne

P.S. - Thank you and Mimi for always loving me for who I am. You both have always loved me and just me. You see me the way I have desperately wanted Father to for longer than I can remember.

January 9th, 2019,
My Dearest, Sweet Suzanne,

I am so sorrowful for your loss. Without sounding presumptuous, I know quite well your Mimi understands completely.

Whenever you start to feel better, that's when I will feel better, too. So it goes for those wired wonderfully in sync. Now, with that assurance, it is only for us to maintain, as we are able, with God's grace, a secure and formidable grounding…. There, I feel even that much better now that we are grounded.

One year from today, every misery in your current family dilemmas will be much improved. It is inevitable. Be patient and let God work.

I cannot cure your pain, but I can love you as no other for as long as forever.

Your Godfather,
Uncle Tommy

P.S.- How much for the moose?

"To love and be loved is to feel the sun from both sides."
-David Viscott

Chapter Forty
Claire

March 7th, 2019,

Dear Uncle Tommy,

How are you doing down in Georgia? The months are cold and the days are short in Pennsylvania.

As you know, Father's last visit did not go as I had hoped. Like his visit before, he waited for a time when Nathan was not around right before it was time for his departure and strong-armed me into what seemed to be a relentless campaign to bring Mother's abuse back into my life.

On the surface, this sounds innocuous—and perhaps, to some extent, it is. For me, however, it was nothing short of devastating. Now that I have finally broken free of Mother's grip on my life, Father has taken an interest in coming to see me two separate times. Each time, I could not have been more excited. It felt like the best of both worlds. Not only was I extricated from Mother's reign, but I was going to be Daddy's little girl again. Well, as you and I both know—it's a hard reality to learn—sometimes, when things seem too good to be true, they are.

The hard truth to process is that it wasn't just Father coming to visit me; Each time, it was Father and an agenda.

The reality that Father could or would not understand my need to be freed from Mother has been much harder to cope with than I imagined. It has crushed me that he had motives for his trips other than spending time with his only living daughter.

In coming to terms with all these feelings, I realized that in each trip, I desperately wanted him to see me—the real me. I wanted him to see me the way you and my friends do. No matter how hard I try, this seems to be a fairy tale. It eviscerates me to the core that he either cannot or will not see me for who I truly am. The hurt is so deep that I had to make a major life decision, and I wanted you to hear it directly from me. It is with a heavy heart that I have chosen to no longer go by my birth name.

I've always said that if I were to have a daughter, I would name her "Claire." The good Lord has blessed me with two amazing boys, so I have decided to take the name for myself. I will never legally change from Suzanne, however, nor will I forsake the name the Lord put in my parents' hearts to call me. This is one way I can continue to honor and love both Mother and Father from afar.

Father could never see me for who I am, so I am giving him Suzanne. Claire is the person I wanted him to see. Claire is also free from a past of abuse. I considered much in making this decision—including my middle name, Elizabeth, which I share with my deceased sister Christine. After much thought and prayer, I have lovingly decided to give the name Elizabeth to Christine in Heaven. It's time just to be me. If the Hunting Island me had a name, I believe it would be Claire. Claire is, indeed, the personification of my innermost spirit that has been waiting to come out.

I'll Love You As Long As Forever,
Claire

"I have called you by your name; You are mine."
-Isaiah 43:1 [NKJV]

Hunting Island Flashback: Still the Same Free Spirit

April 12th, 2019,
To My Dearest Claire (Formerly Suzanne),

Is my Sweet "Suzanne" gone forever? Well, it's easy for me to be sad, but that is my perspective alone.

While I have a personal connection and bond to the name Suzanne, I understand and respect your reasons for no longer going by your birth name.

Wherever thou goest, I am with thee till your personal, wonderful conclusion,

Uncle Tommy

April 9th, 2019,

Dear Uncle Tommy,

I have to share an amazing testimony about my birth name and Claire. Nathan prayed for me one day last week, and he received a word from the Lord. Right as he said the name "Claire," the Lord stopped him in the middle of his sentence just to let him know that Suzanne is the name that he put on Mother and Father's hearts when they were deciding what to name me before I was born. Though I'm still not sure, I wouldn't be surprised if the Lord calls me "Suzanne" one day when I get to Heaven. See, I hold the most profound honor and reverence for this name even though I started going by Claire as part of my healing journey.

Nathan and I were out to lunch yesterday when he told me this story, and now I would like to share with you something additional to show just how compassionate our Lord is. Before Nathan could share this experience with me, I prayed to the Lord. I was in quite a vulnerable place and had deep questions about my name, so I asked God, "If my parents named me Suzanne and I now go by Claire, what do you call me, Lord?" Remember, I asked God this question before I could compassionately hear the truth from my sweet Nathan. This is how tender our Lord was to me: I truly believe that when I asked him that question, he knew that if he told me what he told Nathan, I would not have been able to handle it. I would have freaked out and thought that I needed to un-change my name after many people began to know me as Claire. God knew it would have been a disaster this way, since I had yet to have that conversation with Nathan—the person who knows me best on this planet. So, the Lord was compassionate and tender in his answer. Quite simply, God answered, "I call you daughter."

With Eternal Love,
Claire, daughter of God, and forever in my heart, Suzanne

May 20th, 2019,

Good Ole Uncle Tommy here wishing my sweet, creative, intuitive, free-spirited, Sir Luke-loving family first forever faithful Claire the happiest birthday ever!!!

I'll Love For As Long As Forever,
Uncle Tommy

"The important thing about your lot in life is whether you use it for parking or building."

The Art Heard 'Round the World

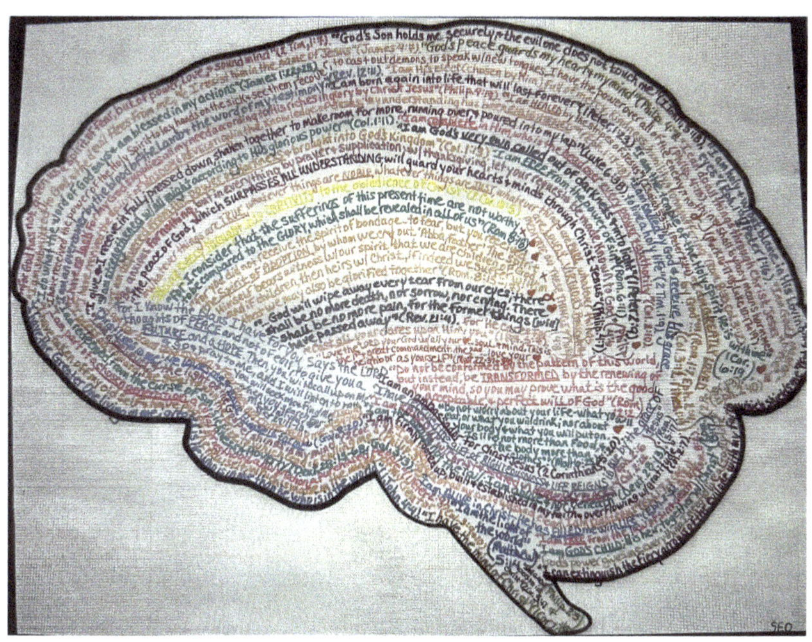

"Each of you should use whatever gift[s] you have received to serve others , as faithful stewards of God's grace in its various forms."
-1 Peter 4:10

In the summer of 2019, I joined a Bible study at our local church. The group did a series called "The Hurt Pocket," which was extremely helpful to me as a survivor of child abuse. Long before I joined this group, I always longed to extensively study specific scriptures on what the Bible says about my identity—who I truly am in Christ. I have heard the expression "who you are in Christ," but I wanted to exclusively study what the Bible says about that and my identity in Christ.

On one of the first weekly Bible study meetings, we were instructed to close our eyes and have a private moment. We stayed in this position of prayer for about five minutes, and I was quite surprised at what I saw when my eyes were closed.

As somebody who managed depression and anxiety for many years, at first, it seemed completely natural to me that I would see a brain when I closed my eyes. *Of course, it's just my depressed brain,* I thought to myself. I saw all the areas of my brain that were wrinkled, but as I continued to look at them, it became clear to me that they were not just wrinkles. Yes, something was distinctly there, but it was not wrinkles. Before I could figure out what I was looking at, the leader directed us to transition out of our position of prayer. If those weren't wrinkles, what were they?

The study began, and within five minutes or so, I had moved on and stopped thinking about the "non-wrinkles" I saw. We learned much about the spiritual damage it can do to hold on to past hurt that night. We were assigned reading to complete before next week and closed in prayer. As we were led to the door, the leader abruptly stopped us and shouted, "Wait!" She had almost forgotten to give us a handout she had planned for this week.

I walked back to the front and reached for the handouts. As I went to the childcare area to pick up my oldest, Luke, I glanced at the paper. Right there in my hands, I clutched a handout titled "Bible Verses That Tell

You Who You Are in Christ." I stopped dead in my tracks. Immediately, the vision I saw earlier when closing my eyes became crystal clear to me. It wasn't wrinkles; it was writing that I saw. The writing was still blurred when I closed my eyes, but it went back to the innate desire of my heart to learn what the Bible says about specifically who I am in Christ. There I stood, holding pages of the lines and lines of Bible verses I didn't realize I had seen in the vision of the brain I saw. The Bible verses were the wrinkles. They were telling me who I am in Christ. God had supernaturally worked through the group leader that night to reveal what I saw in that vision. God was speaking to me to show me exactly what His Word says about who I am in him. I picked up Luke from the childcare center, unable to express in words what I had experienced.

I dreamed about the vision all night. I didn't sleep much. I awoke the following day unable to get it out of my mind. This was too big for writing; this had to be expressed artistically. I drew a rough outline of the human brain. I was not too fond of the first, so I followed an outline from an online diagram. I did it about four or five times until I created an outline I was pleased with. Now, it was time to add the non-wrinkles. I began at the top left lobe. I had all the verses down and decided to alternate wonderful colors for each verse. I changed the orientation of the scriptures several times until I finally found a pattern that worked. Before the day was over, my masterpiece was complete. I had officially completed "The GodBrain."

It wasn't long before I shared my artistic endeavor with good ole Uncle Tommy. Leave it to Uncle Tommy to not only take an interest in my work, but to share it with the world. Before his next mission trip to Kenya, he enlarged, printed, and framed it. Then, he took it with him. While in Kenya, he personally hung it up on the wall of a Kenyan orphanage during his trip. To this day, it still hangs on their walls.

September 20th, 2019,
My Dearest Claire,

Pardon the delay, but please know that you are now quite the artistic celebrity! I have officially hung your creative "brain stem" on the walls of Reformation Life Ministries Orphanage in Kenya from my most recent trip, spreading the word of the Lord. In addition, I have made over fifty copies of your work and distributed them among friends and colleagues. They are quite the rage!

I'll write more soon. No texts; it takes slow Uncle Tommy way too much time and limited energy.

I'll always recall, "I knew her before!"

Ta-Ta & All My Love,
Uncle Tommy

Chapter Forty-Two
Tree of Life

May 24th, 2020

To Sweeeet Claire!

"It's NOT What You Look At That Matters… It's WHAT YOU SEE!!!"

HAPPY BIRTHDAY TO Y-O-U !

I hope you find pleasure with the necklace pendant, "The Tree of Life." It was handcrafted in Poland. Notice it is equally displayed both front & back.

The Tree of Life, for me, is symbolic of its Celtic knot-like entanglements of above-Earth limbs with its below-Earth roots. All are beautifully interwoven together (Knit-Wit comes into similar focus), creating a connectedness that is both spiritual & life-sustaining. It so reminds me of you & your unending passion for everything.

I hope you, Nathan, Luke, & Levi enjoy and celebrate all that makes my dearest Claire a real-life mirror image of "all that is and is within" this exquisite Tree-of-Life!

Bless the days that saw us young and the years that made us wise.

All My Godfatherly Love and Much, Much More,
Uncle Tommy

"Life is but a journey to find our way back home, but we were not created to Journey all alone. God has sent us Jesus to help us on our way, a friend and true companion, so we don't go astray. We are all connected like branches of His tree, I am part of you, and you are part of me. This Tree of Life was planted in Eden long ago, throughout the generations, God's love still makes it grow."

To me, the most beautiful part about the Tree of Life from Uncle Tommy is how we see it come full circle throughout scripture. Like his love for me, it is eternal and encircles The Holy Bible. We see the first mention of the Tree of Life in the Book of Genesis before the fall of man, and it is also seen in the Book of Revelation with the final restoration of Eden. The Tree of Life, like Uncle Tommy's love for me, is the quintessential full circle.

"Now the Lord God had planted a garden in the east, in Eden; … and made all kinds of trees grow out of the ground—trees that were pleasing to the eye and good for food. In the middle of the garden was the tree of life."
-Genesis 2:8 & 9 [NIV]

"Then the angel showed me the river of the water of life, as clear as crystal, flowing from the throne of God and the Lamb down the middle of the great street of the city. On each side of the river stood

the tree of life, bearing twelve crops of fruit, yielding its fruit every month. And the leaves of the tree are for the healing of the nations. No longer will there be any curse. The throne of God and the Lamb will be in the city, and his servants will serve him. They will see his face, and his name will be on their foreheads. There will be no more night. They will not need the lights of a lamp or the light of the sun, for the Lord God will give them light. And they will reign for ever and ever."

-Revelation 22:1-6 [NIV]

Chapter Forty-Three

All Good Things Must Come to an End…

I read the Facebook post at 3:30 P.M. on a Thursday afternoon. Facebook. Tommy had a heart attack. They put a stent in; unresponsive. A Facebook post. As unjust as it seemed, Facebook made the most sense, seeing as I no longer had contact with my biological family. Still, this was Uncle Tommy—my everything, my lifetime advocate. Facebook. I had been through enough not to let that affect me too much. Indeed, I was coping until Operation Fort Knox came into play.

Operation Fort Knox is what I refer to as Tommy's second wife's bizarre attempt to place extreme limitations on who had access to Tommy in the hospital. This wasn't backstage tickets to Aerosmith; it was my beloved Uncle Tommy. If it weren't for one of Brother's fraternity Brothers' Facebook posts, I still would have been in the dark. Thank goodness for that, at least. My husband found out through a separate chain of emails from his Georgia golf friends that Uncle Tommy was at Grady Hospital.

When I first called the hospital, I asked for information on getting in touch with my Godfather, Tommy, and was informed by the woman on the other line that his wife had set up a password and given it to an elite few who made the cut of speaking to him. Weird, but no big deal. I would just email his second wife and ask for the password. Even she was well aware of my and Tommy's special bond.

Things started getting strange when I received the return email from his second wife. "Hello Suzanne." (She must not have received the memo that I go by Claire. No big deal, though). "You have always been very special to Tommy. I am very fortunate for his and your bond. At this time, since his condition is so critical, we are limiting his interactions to close family members only. I'm sure he would have been so glad you reached out."

I replied to her email, "Is his condition critical? Is he going to be okay?"

"The next few days are critical. He is unresponsive with no brain waves."

"I'm sorry, I just want to make sure I understand correctly. He might die, and you are limiting my access to him for his survival chances? Is this a joke? Please let me talk to my Godfather."

No response.

The next day, I received a curious phone call from a stranger (presumably one of Tommy's friends) telling me that I had better leave his second wife alone or else. There was no doubt in my mind he had been speaking to my biological family and came to know me through the worst possible lens. The only updates I received were from his golfing buddy when he posted updates on Facebook. Facebook. It was better than nothing, I thought to myself.

"Even [the]… one who shared my bread, has turned against me."
-Psalm 41:9 (NIV)

It did not take me long to realize that things were ending. The light so brilliantly known as Tommy's life was coming to an end. I pictured him lying there on life support. Status reports indicated he could still hear all those who earned the privilege of phoning or visiting him. I was desperate. In life, they say to choose your battles; I chose this one. I broke through Hell to get to call Tommy. It was worth it.

I ended up emailing his second wife, and as much as I hated to do this (as I could not imagine being in her position), I had to be firm with her this time. This is my Tommy. She just didn't get it. Like all the people who didn't get it—neither did she. She knew Tommy and I were close, but knowing Tommy's deep loyalty, I knew she did not know anything about my child abuse and exactly why it was that Tommy and I were just so close.

My tone was compassionate, yet firm. I'm sure I would get all kinds of colorful phone calls from the same man as before, but I didn't care. "So, here's the deal," I wrote to her. "I'm talking to Tommy. The question is not 'if.' It's simply a matter of 'when' at this point. I'm glad we were able to come to a solution with this. I am available anytime this week. Sincerely, Suzanne."

I would later pay for this, no doubt, but I was in. I penetrated Fort Knox; I got to speak to Tommy before he graduated to glory.

The hour came for which I was allowed to speak my final words to his ears. I had prepared nothing. The way mine and Tommy's spirits flowed, I figured the Holy Spirit would give me the perfect words. Of course, He did.

His second wife answered the phone and handed the receiver to his ear so he could hear my words.

"Heyyyy Tommy, this is Claire, A.K.A. Suzanne in Georgia. I just wanted to tell you that the other day I was thinking about the first job I ever had at age sixteen—do you remember? It was TCBY Yogurt. I believe you are the first person in history to ever 'prank call' someone through a drive-thru. You asked me for a bongo burger in a scruffy cowboy/truck driver voice. I should have known all along it was you, but there I was—my first week on my first job, and I'm sweatin' bullets because I'm trying to find exactly where on our menu it says we serve a concoction known as a 'bongo burger.' I thought I had that baby memorized—what was happening? I was sooo fired. Sure enough, you drove around the corner, and before I could hang up my apron in shame, you revved the engine, and the second I saw your Bronco, I just laughed and said, 'Go figure.'"

The Holy Spirit graciously moved on through my loving words.

"Then, just the other day, I was driving by a Hallmark store, and they must have been doing some early advertising because I saw something about seventy percent off all Kwanzaa cards, and I thought to myself, 'Hey, self—I know someone who knows about this Kwanzaa. In fact, he missed an entire company conference because he got the wrong room and ended up enjoying the company, the food, and eh… the spirits.' To this day, I'll never know what you said to your job to explain your absence, but whatever you said, either it worked, or they didn't care! You will forever be the face of Kwanzaa for me."

The Holy Spirit kept moving.

"And, of course, there's our beloved Hunting Island, which I will forever hold dear in my heart and spirit. Do you remember running on the beach even after Mother told us not to? Later, Brother scolded me for not following Mother's rules, and later, you and I stealthily poured an entire bucket of sand on him. I remember he was ten times messier than both of us combined after we dealt with him!"

The Holy Spirit continued.

"Tommy, in all seriousness, I just want to take a quick minute to tell you how much you mean to me. This is one of those times in life where words fail to justify emotion, but I will try my best anyhow. You have loved me from birth. When I say 'love,' I mean pure love. The love I was deprived of at home, you and Mimi gave to me. That is something that I carry with me every day of my life. Your love has sustained me, and you always pointed me back to God in my life, even in the times when I was most lost. You loved me. You discipled me. You respected me. We laughed together. We cried together. You and I, Tommy, shared life together, and those memories I will hold most precious to me for the rest of my time here. Well, I guess it's time for me to sign off for now. There's no point in telling you goodbye because I will see you again. It's therefore appropriate for me to say, 'See you soon.' You are going to meet Jesus—this is going to be awesome! You will see Mimi, your mom, your dad, your brother Harry, and even your dog Rainbow. Don't you worry a bit about things down here. Everybody is going to be just fine. And yes, Tommy, I will be just fine, too. Long ago, Mimi asked you to watch over me, and I'm here to tell you that you not only fulfilled but greatly surpassed your role. I could not have asked for a better Godfather and lifetime advocate. You believed in me when the entire world turned its back on me. For that, I am eternally grateful. So thank you again, and Tommy… I'll see you real soon."

A few hours later, Tommy left this Earth and graduated onto glory to be with his eternal maker. His body might not have been here anymore, but that was it.

That night as I lay in my bed, I could have sworn that I heard Tommy's signature, hearty laughter amongst the stir of the wind's breeze. His spirit may no longer have been in his body anymore, but one thing's for sure: you can't kill Tommy.

Chapter Forty-Four
The Service

The service was on a Tuesday afternoon in Georgia. Nathan and I took Levi, our youngest, and drove down while Luke stayed with his grandparents. We stopped at a hotel in Kentucky to sleep on Monday night. Tuesday morning, we arrived at Jessica's house. Her son and two daughters had grown so much since I last saw them. The youngest daughter, Victoria, watched Levi during the service. Several of Tommy's lifelong friends spoke during the funeral. Amid my sorrow, I was pleasantly surprised to hear stories of his young adult years, adolescence, and childhood. Unbeknownst to me, many of his older friends and family referred to Tommy as "The Hawk." The Hawk. What a fitting name! He was no wimpy bird, that's for sure. I'll never forget the beautiful picture of Tommy's contagious smile leaning against a crooked tree at that outdoor service. It truly was a beautiful service.

After the funeral, Nathan and I drove back to Jessica's house in ponderous silence. As soon as we got back to her house, Jessica and her friend (also named Jessica) sat on her back porch and we gave a toast to the one and only Tommy Hannah for a life well-lived. After we lowered our glasses and took a sip of our strawberry-flavored wine coolers, the unthinkable happened. Right in front of our eyes and less than five feet away from each of us, an enormous hawk swooped down and gobbled up a squirrel. It wasn't violent, though it was surprising. No, it was just the circle of life. It was no coincidence. God used that incident—the hawk—to show that his death was natural. Death is natural. It's just a part of life.

"To be absent from the body is to be present with the LORD."
-2 Corinthians 5:8

Chapter Forty-Five

My First Birthday Without Tommy

"Blessed are those who mourn, for they will be comforted."
-Matthew 5:4 (NIV)

On May 24th, 2021, I had my first birthday without Tommy. I turned forty years old. Even though I knew he was gone, I helplessly waited like a sad puppy dog for the mail to come that day. I knew they didn't send cards from Heaven, but not hearing from him on my birthday felt so surreal that I waited anyway. Tommy had always been magical to me. If anybody could pull off sending mail from Heaven, it would have been him. When I saw nothing from Tommy for me in the mailbox, I took a somewhat relieving yet sad hit of reality.

I had established they don't send cards from Heaven. But…

Later that day, Nathan took me window shopping for my birthday. He knew I was incredibly down this year. I walked spiritlessly through Hallmark and Target. I think it was official—nothing was going to cheer me up. Before I suggested we return home, we decided to stop at a mom-

and-pop handcrafted arts store. The décor was filled with burlap items and sunflowers decked out for the summer. I almost felt my spirits lift slightly, but I knew it wouldn't last. Before I turned around to motion to Nathan to leave, I stopped dead in my tracks when I saw a certain card. It was a coral color with a pattern of white circles in the background. In the foreground, a beautiful, magical woman was drawn. She had rainbow-streaked hair; she wore a crown on top of her head; and she wore a cross around her neck that was held up by a multicolored, beaded chain.

On the inside, it said, "When the burdens of life seem too heavy and you feel that you cannot go on… Remember whose daughter you are and adjust your crown."

On the back?

The back of the card indicated that it was made in St. **Thomas,** Pennsylvania.

Apparently, they do deliver mail from Heaven….

Forgiveness - The Spark That Put it All in Motion

I had been sitting on this book idea for two years after Tommy's passing. I had a lifetime's worth of letters, and I had my idea in place. I knew what I wanted to write, but I couldn't grasp my momentum. I couldn't get started. It wasn't exactly "writer's block"—it was something more profound than that. I was spiritually blocked.

It wasn't until the Spring of 2023 when a dear friend sat me down and told me the cold, hard truth that I needed (but didn't want to) hear. I needed to clean up my side of the street before I could walk in alignment with God's perfect plan for my life. It wasn't just enough to forgive Mother and Father in my heart. They needed to *know* that I forgave them. Simply put, I had to write them a letter of forgiveness.

"When you stand praying, if you hold anything against anyone, forgive them so that your Father in heaven may forgive you your sins."
-Mark 11:25 (NIV)

Unforgiveness is a blessing blocker. While we know as born-again believers that Jesus has already forgiven us of our past, present, and even future sins, I think there's something powerful to be said here in this scripture. From a salvation standpoint, yes, we have been forgiven, but it does not mean we will always walk in God's perfect will for us on Earth. I truly believe that is what it means when we read, "...so that your Father in heaven may forgive your sins." Yes, you have been forgiven in the sense of going to Heaven, but God has so much more for you right now. Forgive others so he can bless you!

I had just finished watching the movie *I Can Only Imagine*, which is about a boy who had been abused by his father growing up but he forgives him as an adult. It was go-time.

I mailed my letter to them on a Friday in July of 2023, which was coincidentally the fifteen-year anniversary of the date Nathan and I first met on my first day of work at the engineering firm in Georgia. The day I unknowingly met the love of my life while secretly living in an extended-stay motel.

The following Monday, this book hit the ground running. Here I am, less than six months later, and I'm finishing it up. Sometimes, when the blessing hits you, it moves you at a speed beyond your wildest dreams.

For years, I swore I would never give Mother and Father a free pass for the things they did to me. I am honored to state that I have since changed this viewpoint. It's not my job to judge them, but it is my honor and privilege to forgive them. Do they deserve it? No, but I didn't deserve God's forgiveness either, and he still gave it to me. Who am I to withhold that which I have already freely been given by my Father in Heaven?

To this day, I still pray that Mother, Father, and Brother can find Jesus and He can transform their lives.

Mother never dimmed my light. I still kept shining. Because I live out that light that shines in my spirit, it is wonderful to say how deeply I forgive her. I hold no charge against her. After all these years, I finally changed my mind. Yes, they get a free pass. I completely and wholeheartedly forgive them. They are released in love.

Chapter Forty-Seven

The Last Letter

Midway through the book, I was still frantically searching for Tommy's last letter. The final one he sent me before he went to be with the Lord. The chapters were outlined, the letters were all organized, and I had my flow down, but I still could not find the last letter. It felt like I lost him all over again. Even though it was just a physical thing, it meant the world to me. I had lost something that could not be replaced. I felt like I was grieving all over again.

In October of 2023, I finally resigned to stop looking. In an air of defeat, I placed all the letters back in their box and went to my closet to put them back. They had been returned. About a week later, I was back in my closet searching for a long-lost dress when I noticed a white sliver of paper sticking out of a sweatshirt pocket. *Don't get your hopes up, Claire; don't get your hopes up.*

I shut my eyes tightly as I pulled the paper out of its hiding crevice. It felt like an eternity until I slowly started to peek. First the right eye, then the left, and there it sat in my hands—the last letter Tommy had written me in his lifetime.

"Every good and perfect gift is from above." -James 1:17 (NIV)

March 7th, 2021,
My Dearest Claire,

"The next time you refuse to sing, because you'll never fill a
Stadium, or decline the joy of dance for fear of looking
Ridiculous, or resist the risk of a new adventure for fear of the
Unknown, or you dim your shine because you're not completely
Healed and whole.

Just remember…

A bird doesn't sing because it's talented,
A bird sings because it has a song.

The moon doesn't only shine when it's whole;
It can show up with a single sliver of itself
And still light the entire night sky."

Take care of yourself, my Sweet Daughter of Eve.

About the Author

Rising above a life of child abuse, Claire Ostrander surpasses unimaginable odds and tells the heartwarming story of her Godfather's love and the decision to follow Christ in her inspiring memoir, *Sweet Daughter of Eve.* Ostrander's decision to follow Jesus and break the generational cycle of child abuse has now inspired her to become a catalyst to those suffering in silence from abuse. A graduate of Kennesaw State University, Ostrander received her B.A. in English in 2008. When she least expected it, the Lord brought her the love of her life, and she and her husband were married in 2010. Since then, they have brought two beautiful boys into this world. Her children represent the first generation of a new legacy of Christ, hope, and love.